Wake Up to the
WORD

365 DEVOTIONS TO
Inspire You Each Day

JOYCE MEYER

Faith
Words

LARGE PRINT

FaithWords
Hachette Book Group
1290 Avenue of the Americas, New York, NY 10104

faithwords.com

twitter.com/faithwords

First Edition: October 2016

FaithWords is a division of Hachette Book Group, Inc. The FaithWords name and logo are trademarks of Hachette Book Group, Inc.

The publisher is not responsible for websites (or their content) that are not owned by the publisher.

The Hachette Speakers Bureau provides a wide range of authors for speaking events. To find out more, go to www.hachettespeakersbureau.com or call (866) 376-6591.

Unless otherwise noted, Scriptures are taken from *The Amplified Bible, Classic Edition* copyright © 1965, 1987 by The Zondervan Corporation.

Scripture quotations marked (AMP) are taken from *The Amplified Bible* copyright © 2015 by The Lockman Foundation. Used by permission.

Scripture quotations marked (NIV) are taken from the *Holy Bible: New International Version* ®. Copyright © 1973, 1978, 1984 by International Bible Society. Used by permission of Zondervan Publishing House. All rights reserved.

Scripture quotations marked (MSG) are taken from *The Message*. Copyright © 1993, 1994, 1995, 1996, 2000, 2001, 2002. Used by permission of NavPress Publishing Group.

Scripture quotations marked (NKJV) are taken from the *New King James Version*. Copyright © 1979, 1980, 1982 by Thomas Nelson, Inc., Publishers.

Scripture quotations marked (NLT) are taken from the *Holy Bible*, New Living Translation, Copyright © 1996. Used by permission of Tyndale House Publishers, Inc., Wheaton, Illinois 60189. All rights reserved.

ISBN: 978-1-4555-5995-4 (paper over board hardcover), 978-1-4555-5997-8 (ebook), 978-1-4555-5998-5 (large print)

Printed in the United States of America

LSC-C

10 9 8 7 6 5 4 3 2

Introduction

Words are powerful. With one word, God can change our lives and we can help change the course of someone's day. Within one word, we can find encouragement and hope.

Proverbs 25:11 says, "A word fitly spoken and in due season is like apples of gold in settings of silver." This verse is the inspiration behind *Wake Up to the Word*.

This 365-day devotional features one word for each day of the year, a definition of that word, a Bible verse, and a Bible-based encouragement. *Wake Up to the Word* not only takes you deeper into God's Word but it is a great resource if you're looking for a quick word of encouragement each morning that will provide something to meditate on throughout the day.

I hope you enjoy reading this book as much as I enjoyed working on it. I pray it will be a blessing in your life.

Wake Up to the
WORD

Determined

Having a firm or fixed purpose; or manifesting a firm resolution, as a determined countenance.

One of the great benefits of following Jesus is knowing that with Him you can't lose. Because He is with you, no matter what you face, you can overcome. Things won't always be easy, but if you are determined to keep moving forward, you will make progress.

In your relationships, your finances, your career, and your emotional well-being the only way you can lose is if you give up. So be determined today, even in the toughest circumstances.

God is with you (see Joshua 1:9), and He has promised to never leave your side (see Matthew 28:20). If you'll hold on to those promises, you'll live a bold, confident, determined life.

> *And let us not lose heart and grow weary and*
> *faint in acting nobly and doing right, for*
> *in due time and at the appointed season we*
> *shall reap, if we do not loosen and relax our*
> *courage and faint.*   GALATIANS 6:9

Accepted

Kindly received; regarded; agreed to; understood; received as a bill of exchange

---

Have you ever felt rejected, unwanted, or out of place?

None of us experiences acceptance from everyone in our lives. In fact, many experience a type of rejection that damages our souls. We may believe we are flawed if people have rejected us, and, therefore, we mistakenly decide we are worthless.

But this is not true. Don't let someone else's behavior, words, or actions toward you make you feel inferior. The truth is that God created you and He delights in you. He loves you, and He will never reject you.

You can live beyond your feelings—you can move past the pain of rejection. You are unconditionally loved and completely accepted by your Heavenly Father.

All whom My Father gives (entrusts) to Me will come to Me; and the one who comes to Me I will most certainly not cast out [I will never, no never, reject one of them who comes to Me]. JOHN 6:37

Righteousness

**Applied to God, the perfection
or holiness of His nature; exact
rectitude; faithfulness**

There are two kinds of righteousness. The
first is a righteousness that we try to earn
through our good works. The second is
the righteousness that is given as a free gift
to those who sincerely believe in Jesus.

The first kind of righteousness causes
struggle and frustration and can never
truly be attained. But righteousness through
Christ allows you to rest in God and
appreciate His love and mercy.

My own struggle to keep the rules and
earn righteousness was intense and caused

me many years of agony. I was trying to get to God through good behavior, yet I always fell short.

But Jesus invites all of us to give up striving for works-based righteousness in our own strength so we can receive righteousness by faith in Him. Choose to receive His gift of righteousness today.

But to one who, not working [by the Law], trusts (believes fully) in Him Who justifies the ungodly, his faith is credited to him as righteousness (the standing acceptable to God).   ROMANS 4:5

Creative

Having the power to create

God is amazingly creative, and His Spirit dwells in you. You were created in His image, so that means you, too, are creative.

Do you live a life of boring sameness because you are afraid to try anything new? A great deal of creativity lies within you, and God wants to show you how to tap into it and express it without fear.

God must enjoy variety or He would not have created each of us to be so unique in our individuality. We often hear, "Variety is the spice of life." Sometimes even a slight deviation from sameness is refreshing.

Always walk in wisdom, but don't ever

be afraid to step out and try something new. Use the creativity God has uniquely given you!

And He has filled him with the Spirit of God, with ability and wisdom, with intelligence and understanding, and with knowledge and all craftsmanship, to devise artistic designs.

EXODUS 35:31–32

Gladness

Joy, or a moderate degree of joy and exhilaration; peace of mind; cheerfulness

---

The reality of what it means to be a forgiven and adored child of God should give us unimaginable joy. So why are so many Christians miserable?

I believe it is because they do not understand the reality of being a new creation in Christ and the inheritance that is ours in Him. A struggle or difficulty distracts them, and they simply forget the promises of God for their lives. They end up sad instead of glad.

Jesus did not die to give you a "down"

life—He is your glory and lifter of your head! (See Psalm 3:3.) God has given you everything you need to enjoy Him and to enjoy yourself and the life He has given you!

Your joy is in knowing Christ and the hope that He offers us. Take hold of it and walk in gladness.

> *You have turned my mourning into dancing for me; You have put off my sackcloth and girded me with gladness.* PSALM 30:11

Brave

Courageous; bold; daring; intrepid; fearless of danger; as a brave warrior

---

The only way to conquer fear is to confront it and to do the thing you are afraid of. If you don't, you will be a prisoner all your life.

When we do confront things, we always find that the worst part of the fear was in our minds, and the reality of the thing wasn't as bad as we had imagined.

If you truly want to be free, understand that facing a fear is better than being afraid all your life. Fear is a terrible burden to live with.

Bravery to overcome life's fears comes when you ask God for His help, trust He is with you, and face that fear head-on.

For God did not give us a spirit of timidity (of cowardice, of craven and cringing and fawning fear), but [He has given us a spirit] of power and of love and of calm and well-balanced mind and discipline and self-control.   2 TIMOTHY 1:7

Receive

**To take, as a thing offered or sent;
to accept**

"To get" means to obtain by struggle and effort, but "to receive" means to simply take in what is being offered. Our relationship with God was never intended to be complicated and based upon our own works. The more we learn how to receive from God by faith, the simpler and more enjoyable our walk with Him becomes.

You can keep your relationship with God simple by receiving His unconditional love and believing His Word no matter what you think or how you feel. You can receive by faith all that He offers, even though you know full well that you don't deserve it. And you can choose to lean on, trust in, and rely on Him to meet every need you have instead of worrying and trying to figure things out.

And with His help (grace), you can obey Him and grow in spiritual maturity by knowing His will and receiving His best for your life!

But to as many as did receive and welcome Him, He gave the authority (power, privilege, right) to become the children of God, that is, to those who believe in (adhere to, trust in, and rely on) His name.   JOHN 1:12

Mercy

**That benevolence, mildness or
tenderness of heart that disposes
a person to overlook injuries or to
treat an offender better than he
deserves**

No matter how hard we try to do what is
right, we are always going to have some
flaws. But in our flaws, God demonstrates
His amazing mercy in our lives. And every
time we experience the mercy of God, we
are drawn closer to Him.

Don't keep score of your mistakes any
longer. If God isn't counting, why are you?
The score doesn't matter, because whatever you do right, God gets the glory for

it—and whatever you do wrong, only God can fix it. So whether you do right or wrong, you are in Christ and you belong to Him.

Simply love Him the best you can and trust Him to take care of all things. Be happy in God's love and acceptance, enjoy His mercy and forgiveness, grow in His grace, and be delighted in His favor.

It is because of the Lord's mercy and loving-kindness that we are not consumed, because His [tender] compassions fail not.

LAMENTATIONS 3:22

Imagine

To form ideas or representations in the mind, by modifying and combining our conceptions

---

We all have an area of our thought life called imagination. That's where we see mental images of how we believe things are. If you see yourself as a failure when you're actually a forgiven child of God, then you have an imagination that needs to be renewed.

Your imaginings and mind prepare you for action. They can prepare you for success or failure, joy or misery—the choice is up to you. You can learn to see yourself as God does. Then you will see His good plan for you come to pass.

If you often think about your past mistakes, they handicap you as you try to enter the future God has planned for you. No matter what you have done in the past, ask the Lord to help you learn to see yourself as a new creature in Christ (see 2 Corinthians 5:17).

Now to him who is able to do immeasurably more than all we ask or imagine, according to his power that is at work within us…

EPHESIANS 3:20 (NIV)

Future

Time to come; a time subsequent to the present

We would all like to know what the future holds for us. God does have a good plan for each of us, but we have to be willing to follow His plan, rather than going our own way in order to experience it.

God wants us to live the good life that He has prearranged and made ready for us to live. In order to press on, we must forget what lies behind us. Your future has no room in it for bad feelings from your past. Take the good things from the past and the lessons you've learned along with you, but let go of anything that is holding you back or keeping you stuck in fear or insecurity of any kind.

You can have hope instead of hopelessness. Start believing today that your future is filled with good things and refuse to settle for less than God's best for you.

For I know the thoughts and plans that I have for you, says the Lord, thoughts and plans for welfare and peace and not for evil, to give you hope in your final outcome.

JEREMIAH 29:11

Change

To cause to turn or pass from one state to another; to alter, or make different

_____

When I began studying God's Word more than forty years ago, I thought, *How can one person need as much changing as I do?* Now, after all these years, I wonder, *How can one person have changed so much?*

I also wonder if the process is ever done, because I still need changing every day. Forty years ago, I was frustrated by that, but today it doesn't disturb me at all. I thank God when He shows me an area of my life that needs improvement; I receive it as loving instruction from Him and trust Him to change me.

If you want to see change in your life, God will change you by His Holy Spirit. He also uses His Word and your experiences in life. These are all important, and they all work together to mold you into the image of Christ.

Be thankful for and embrace the change that God sends your way and believe that as you apply His Word and principles, He will work all things together for good in your life. (See Romans 8:28.)

Bring forth fruit that is consistent with repentance [let your lives prove your change of heart].   MATTHEW 3:8

Trust

Confidence; a reliance or resting of the mind on the integrity, veracity, justice, friendship or other sound principle of another person

---

Trust is a beautiful thing. And it's something we decide to do, not something we necessarily feel.

Trust is what makes a relationship comfortable. We put our money in a bank because it has a good reputation and we decide to trust our money to it. God has a much better reputation than even the best bank in the world, so we can surely decide to deposit our lives with Him and put our total trust in His Word.

You can trust God to always understand everything about you, because He understands you better than you understand yourself. You can trust Him to never reject you, to always be there for you, to be on your side and to love you unconditionally. He is merciful, long-suffering with your weaknesses and more patient than you can even fathom.

What time I am afraid, I will have confidence in and put my trust and reliance in You.

PSALM 56:3

Surrender

To yield to the power of another

I am learning to love the word "surrender."

It means that I stop wrestling with God and resisting His will. I may not understand all that He is doing or the way He is doing it, but I can surrender. I can yield to Him, and so can you. Some of the things that frustrate us in life would stop hurting if we would embrace them—trusting that God knows best—rather than constantly resisting them.

Anytime you resist what only God can control, your spirit is not at rest. But when you choose to walk in step with Him, you will find yourself in complete peace. You do not need to be afraid to surrender to God. He always has your best interest in mind.

> *So then, any of you who does not forsake*
> *(renounce, surrender claim to, give up, say*
> *good-bye to) all that he has cannot be My*
> *disciple.*   LUKE 14:33

Goodness

The state of being good; the physical qualities that constitute value, excellence, or perfection

---

God is good, without exception. In other words, He is good to everyone, all the time. His goodness radiates from Him. If you were abused or abandoned in your childhood or hurt badly by someone in your life, you might be wondering, *If God is good, why didn't He deliver me from those circumstances?* I understand that question because I've asked it many times myself.

I don't always get all the answers I would like to have, but I have learned to trust God even when I don't understand.

Everything that has happened in your life may not be good, but God is good, and He can work everything out for good if you will trust Him. God's entire motive and purpose is to be good to you if you will only receive it from Him.

But when the goodness and loving-kindness of God our Savior to man [as man] appeared, He saved us.   TITUS 3:4–5

Growth

Advancement; progress; improvement

When we receive Christ as our Savior, our spirit is saved and we are born again. Our spirit is made holy and God comes to dwell in us. The Word of God, when it is received and becomes rooted in our hearts, has the power to change us from the inside out. As we study God's Word and meditate on His promises, spiritual growth happens.

Spiritual maturity doesn't develop from mere church attendance, giving large sums of money, or serving on a committee—it develops from learning and applying the Word of God in your everyday life.

While it is good to attend church, give, and serve, it is your personal relationship with God and following the Holy Spirit that brings about maturity. True spiritual growth comes when you apply God's Word in every situation and step beyond your comfort zone and trust Him in all things, especially the ones you cannot control.

But grow in grace (undeserved favor, spiritual strength) and recognition and knowledge and understanding of our Lord and Savior Jesus Christ (the Messiah).   2 PETER 3:18

Safe

Free from danger of any kind

One of our most urgent needs in life is to feel safe. Maybe you (or someone you know) grew up with angry, absent, or abusive parents and even now you often don't feel safe. For many, there is a feeling of impending doom or danger hanging over them most of the time.

But God wants us to feel safe with Him. He is a loving Father—kind, forgiving, generous, long-suffering, patient, and faithful. God loves to make wrong things right, and He promises to do it for you. He wants you to know you are safe in His arms.

If your earthly father was absent, you need to know that Father God is omnipresent—He is everywhere all the time. You will never be anywhere that God is not with you. You can fully trust God to keep you safe. Let Him replace your fear and brokenness with His peace and comfort. You are safe with Him.

The name of the Lord is a strong tower; the righteous run to it and are safe.

PROVERBS 18:10 (NKJV)

Love

In a general sense to be pleased with; to regard with affection

---

To many, the words "I love you" are mere words with no meaning. However, when God says that He loves us, He means it in every way that is important and vital to us. His love always moves Him to action on our behalf.

God's love (agape) seeks the welfare of all and works no ill toward any. It seeks an opportunity to do good to all men. God's love is the love of a perfect being toward entirely unworthy objects (us).

God's Word states that He loves us because He wants to, and it is His kind intent. God loves because He must—it is who He is. God is love!

Receive God's unconditional love today. It is the foundation of your relationship with Him. Yes, and a thousand times yes— GOD LOVES YOU!

> *And we have known and believed the love*
> *that God has for us. God is love, and he who*
> *abides in love abides in God, and God*
> *in him.* 1 JOHN 4:16 (NKJV)

Clearly

Plainly; evidently; fully

I have dry eyes and frequently have to put thick eye drops in them for moisture. After I use them, my vision is blurry for a while and I can't see clearly. I can see, but everything I see is distorted.

That is the way we see the world and ourselves when we are operating out of a root of rejection or feelings of worthlessness—our perception of reality is blurred.

The way you view everything in life is determined by your inner thoughts. You see through your own thoughts, and if those thoughts are inaccurate, then you see things in a wrong way.

God wants to remove the wrong perceptions that color your thinking and to replace them with right, godly perceptions about yourself and others. This is done as your mind is renewed through studying God's Word.

Now I know in part (imperfectly), but then I shall know and understand fully and clearly, even in the same manner as I have been fully and clearly known and understood [by God].   1 CORINTHIANS 13:12

Victory

The advantage or superiority gained over spiritual enemies, over passions and appetites, or over temptations, or in any struggle or competition

---

I believe God has a gold-medal story for each of us. He desires for you to enjoy a life that overcomes obstacles and seizes opportunities. But there is an essential key to victory: You have to move past your past.

There are many people who aren't experiencing victory today because they are focused on yesterday. When they close their eyes, they don't see their dreams for tomorrow; they only see the devastation of yesterday.

But I'm here to tell you that you can walk in victory every day of your life. Victory comes when you take your eyes off yourself and place them solely on Jesus.

God has taken care of your past, and a wonderful future awaits you. He is rewriting your story and reshaping your identity. Claim your victory!

But thanks be to God, Who gives us the victory [making us conquerors] through our Lord Jesus Christ.   1 CORINTHIANS 15:57

Time

A particular portion or part of duration, whether past, present or future

---

Do you ever feel that life is incomplete because something you have desperately longed for hasn't happened? All you wanted was a happy marriage, but he left you. You dreamed your whole life of having a baby, but you haven't conceived. You thought you'd be together forever, but the person you loved died. You tried and tried to heal a relationship, but it remains broken. You gave years to a career, but it hasn't panned out.

Perhaps you feel that it is too late for you to truly enjoy your life, but that is just not true. I want to tell you that your "too late" is God's "just in time." He loves to do things in your life that man assumes are impossible. God's thoughts are not your thoughts, and His ways are not your ways (see Isaiah 55:8). In other words, God's plan is different from yours, and God's timetable is different from your timetable. With Him, there is no such thing as too late. God always shows up at just the right time!

To everything there is a season, and a time for every matter or purpose under heaven.

ECCLESIASTES 3:1

Identity

The distinct personality of an individual regarded as a persisting entity

---

The best way to defeat a lie is to know and speak the truth. The next time the enemy lies to you about who you are and accuses you of being unworthy, declare your identity in Christ. Answer him by saying:

- I am the righteousness of God in Jesus Christ
  (2 Corinthians 5:21).
- I am forgiven of all my sins
  (Ephesians 1:7).

- I am born of God, and the evil one does not touch me (1 John 5:18).
- I am a conqueror through Him Who loves me (Romans 8:37).

Those are just a few of the many things that identify you as a child of God. You are not identified by your background, your level of education, your mistakes, or your friends—you are identified by what God has done for you and in you.

Live out your God-created identity. Live generously and graciously toward others, the way God lives toward you.

MATTHEW 5:48 (MSG)

Strength

Power of vigor of any kind

Sometimes the obstacles we face in life surprise us, zap our strength, and steal our joy. Not only do difficult circumstances hit us when we're not expecting them, but they can hit us when we're in our most vulnerable state.

This is what causes many people to give up. They decide it's too much to overcome. But that's not God's plan for His people. And that's not God's plan for you! You don't have to be overwhelmed by the pressures of life.

You might think, *I'm just tired. It seems like I don't have the strength for another battle.* Well, I'm glad you realize you don't have the strength for the battle—because if you try to fight in your own strength, you'll lose every time. The only way you are going to really, truly live in victory is by trusting God with your battles and in your times of weakness. When you do, He will give you all the strength you need.

> *He gives power to the faint and weary, and to him who has no might He increases strength [causing it to multiply and making it to abound].*   ISAIAH 40:29

Dream

To think; to imagine

Each of us should have a dream and go after that dream with all our hearts. Dreams are different from plans. Plans are manageable opportunities, but dreams are often too big to be managed. You plan to assemble a model airplane, but you dream to fly.

Dreams always require faith because they are bigger than you or your ability to accomplish them. That is why I believe faith-filled dreams are so important. When you dream a big dream for God, you will need to become totally dependent on Him to bring it to pass.

All dreamers come to the point where they stop and say, "Lord, this is the dream I believe You've given me, but I don't know how to make it happen. I need You to make this dream come true. I need You to lead the way."

Trust God's timing and diligently take each step He guides you to take. You will see your God-ordained dreams come to pass if you don't give up.

Hope deferred makes the heart sick, but a dream fulfilled is a tree of life.

PROVERBS 13:12 (NLT)

Care

Caution; a looking to; regard; attention or heed, with a view to safety or protection

---

If we don't take good care of our bodies, our spirit and soul will be less effective. If we rarely exercise, rest, or eat properly, we can adversely affect our health. Each part of our being—spirit, soul and body—is important and needs proper care.

I have discovered that when I feel tired and worn-out, I don't want to maintain the spiritual discipline that I should to stay strong in my spirit and soul. Good physical health and energy help us in every way.

Your body is the residence of your spirit

and soul; it is the house they dwell in while on this earth. God's Word says that your body is the temple of God—I encourage you to take care of it each and every day.

Do you not know that your body is the temple (the very sanctuary) of the Holy Spirit Who lives within you, Whom you have received [as a Gift] from God? You are not your own.

1 CORINTHIANS 6:19

Reward

Recompense, or equivalent return for good done, for kindness, for services and the like

---

God desires that we be diligent and committed at all times to doing the right thing. Doing something right once doesn't solve our problems, but consistency will ultimately bring great benefits.

When we tire of doing the right thing while we're waiting for right results that have not manifested themselves yet, we should always remember that God promises us rewards for our diligence. I like to say, "Hold on! Payday is coming!"

God is faithful, and what He promises

to do, He always does. He has good plans
for you and He may not be early in deliver-
ing your rewards, but He won't be late!

   Your labor in the Lord will never be over-
looked or forgotten (see Hebrews 6:10).

*He is the rewarder of those who earnestly and
diligently seek Him.*   HEBREWS 11:6

Courage

Bravery; intrepidity; that quality of mind that enables men to encounter danger and difficulties with firmness or without fear or depression of spirits

---

Judges chapter 20 tells the story of the Israelites losing battles on two consecutive days. Rather than give up after their first defeat, they "took courage and strengthened themselves."

The men of Israel had a choice to make after their defeats: Would they try again, believing that with God they wouldn't fail, or would they take the easy way out and give up? It takes courage to keep pressing on when you have already experienced what appears to be failure, but we see in God's Word that when the Israelites kept going, trusting Him, they ended up victorious.

Many people live unfulfilled lives because they let one or two failures defeat them. I like to say that we are not failures just because we fail at something. Nobody is a failure until he or she quits trying. Be courageous—keep on trying.

But the people, the men of Israel, took courage and strengthened themselves and again set their battle line.   JUDGES 20:22

Passionate

**Expressing strong emotion;
animated**

Living with purpose is an important step in knowing and understanding what God wants to do with us. When we understand our purpose, we have a road map in front of us that's a useful and necessary guide.

However, if purpose is our journey and destination, then passion is the fuel that's going to get us there and it's vital for us to keep that fuel in well-stocked supply.

Life without passion is a life without joy. We all need a reason to get up every day and, with God's help, we can find that passion—that spark that keeps us motivated. We can be enthusiastic and full of joy!

The human heart was made for passion— for strong desire to reach for something more. This is why you can go through life celebrating rather than complaining. God has a great plan for your life. That's something to get excited about!

Never lag in zeal and in earnest endeavor; be aglow and burning with the Spirit, serving the Lord.   ROMANS 12:11

Thought

Idea; conception

_____

One of my favorite things to say is, "Where the mind goes, the man follows," because the way you think determines the way you live.

If you think you're going to be defeated, then you're going to have an attitude that leads to defeat. But if you choose to think about God's promises, you're going to have a faith-filled, expectant attitude.

Yesterday, you may have let your mind focus on the negative—what you can't do, how badly you've messed up, all the things that could go wrong—but today you can submit your mind to the Word of God.

You can actually choose the thoughts you are going to dwell on.

With the help of the Holy Spirit, you can change your thoughts today. You can choose a better, more positive, more fulfilling life.

But we have the mind of Christ (the Messiah) and do hold the thoughts (feelings and purposes) of His heart.

1 CORINTHIANS 2:16

Success

**The favorable or prosperous
termination of any thing
attempted**

Our ultimate success and value in life is
not found in climbing what the world calls
the ladder of success. Our success is not in
a job promotion, a bigger house, a better-
looking car, or elite social circles.

True success is knowing God and the
power of His resurrection. It's knowing
that He loves you unconditionally and
that you are made acceptable in Jesus, the
Beloved Son of God, Who died for you, to
pay for your sins.

Real success is allowing God to help

you be the best you can be, but never having to be better than someone else to prove
that you are valuable.

Roll your works upon the Lord [commit and
trust them wholly to Him; He will cause your
thoughts to become agreeable to His will,
and] so shall your plans be established and
succeed.   PROVERBS 16:3

Whole

Complete; entire; not defective or imperfect

Childhood traumas have a way of lingering in our minds; we often wince at the memories. For many people, these memories hold them back in life.

But that doesn't have to be you. The good news is that in Christ you are not broken or fractured—you are healed and whole. You can shake off the effects of past pain and go on to do great things.

Each time you are reminded of how you were wounded, think about how much God loves you. You're not damaged because someone or something hurt you—you are not inferior. You are a loved, redeemed, restored child of God.

Knowing how valuable you are to God, and that He has an amazing plan for your life, will enable you to overcome painful memories and embrace the love and joy of God that are yours today.

Let the redeemed of the Lord say so, whom He has delivered from the hand of the adversary.

PSALM 107:2

Diligent

Steady in application to business; constant in effort or exertion to accomplish what is undertaken

---

Many people are unhappy because they only want to do things that are easy or convenient. This saddens me because these people often cheat themselves out of the rewards God has for them simply because they want to avoid difficulty.

If we are willing to let God help us do our best, we will reap great benefits.

God wants to bless you in many ways. Sometimes you may go through difficulties first, but there is always blessing on the other side. Remember, you never have to do it in your own strength—you can always rely on His strength to see you through. If you refuse to give up, you'll overcome every challenge and receive God's best for your life.

> *Therefore, brethren, be even more diligent to make your call and election sure, for if you do these things you will never stumble.*
>
> 2 PETER 1:10 (NKJV)

All

Every one, or the whole number of particulars

Notice that the above verse doesn't say, "In a *few* of your ways acknowledge Him," and it doesn't say, "In *most* of your ways acknowledge Him." The Word of God ways, "In *all* your ways, know, recognize, and acknowledge Him."

That means nothing is off-limits. Good or bad, clean or dirty, lost or found, every part of your life can be given to God. You can trust Him with your life, even when you're stuck in a situation and you're not sure how you got into it and certainly don't know how to get out of it!

Don't listen to the lies of the enemy. You don't have to hide from God out of fear that He is angry or disappointed, and you don't have to find a way to move forward without Him. You can trust God to be with you and to show you the way in all things and at all times.

Lean on, trust in, and be confident in the Lord with all your heart... In all your ways know, recognize, and acknowledge Him, and He will direct and make straight and plain your paths.   PROVERBS 3:5–6

Tenderhearted

Having great sensibility; susceptible of impressions or influence

---

I can truthfully say that some of the deepest hurts I have experienced in my life have come from harsh, religious, rule-keeping people who did not walk in love.

If we think we have no faults, then we find fault with almost everyone else. But if we know we need forgiveness, then we will be able to forgive others. If we know we need mercy and long-suffering patience from God, we will be able to give mercy to others and be patient with them, also.

We can't give away something we don't

have, so we need to receive God's love, forgiveness, kindness, mercy, and everything else we need from Him. Tenderhearted people understand what God has so graciously done for them, and they can't wait to share the love of God with those around them.

And become useful and helpful and kind to one another, tenderhearted (compassionate, understanding, loving-hearted), forgiving one another [readily and freely], as God in Christ forgave you.   EPHESIANS 4:32

New

Recently produced by change; as a new life

It's so amazing to realize that when we give our lives to Christ, He takes us just as we are and in exchange, gives us His nature, making us a new creation. It's just the beginning of a lifelong journey we take with Him to become everything God created us to be.

In this process, God doesn't give us a list of rules to follow and then stand on the sidelines watching us fail, but He gives us a new heart and then helps us do all that He has given us a desire to do.

We can learn to depend entirely on

Jesus to give us right standing with God and to help us do what is right in His sight. We can form the habit of leaning on God in all things.

The cardinal guideline for the Christian who wants to be what God wants him to be is, "Apart from Me…you can do nothing" (John 15:5). Abide in Christ as the branch abides in the vine, continually receiving new life that produces new growth.

> *Therefore, if anyone is in Christ, he is a new creation; old things have passed away; behold, all things have become new.*
>
> 2 CORINTHIANS 5:17 (NKJV)

Unoffended

Not offended; not having taken offense

One of our first responses when someone hurts or offends us can be to pray: "God, I choose to believe the best. My feelings are hurt, but You can heal me. I refuse to be angry; I refuse to be offended." It's important to be firm in your determination that you will not be offended because offense is a trap that pulls us away from God, His people, and His principles.

The word *offense* comes from the Greek word *skandalon*. A skandalon was the part of an animal trap that held the bait; its purpose was to lure a victim. Offense is bait that will lure us into a trap of full-blown bitterness, resentment, and unforgiveness.

When you are tempted to be offended, choose to forgive right away. Don't give the bitterness you feel a chance to take root in your life. Choosing to live without offense is one of the wisest choices you can make. If you need to forgive someone, today is the best day to do it!

Good sense makes a man restrain his anger,
and it is his glory to overlook a transgression
or an offense.　　　　　PROVERBS 19:11

Freely

Spontaneously; without constraint or persuasion

When the Lord, in the person of the Holy Sprit, comes to dwell in our heart, He brings love with Him, because God is love (see 1 John 4:8).

It's important to ask what we are doing with the love of God that has been freely given to us. Are we rejecting it because we don't think we are valuable enough to be loved? Do we believe God is like other people who have rejected and hurt us? Or are we receiving His love by faith, believing that He is greater than our failures and weaknesses?

With God's help, we can love ourselves—not in a selfish way, but in a balanced, godly way; a way that simply affirms God's creation as essentially good and right. God's plan is this: for us to receive His love freely, love ourselves in a godly way, generously love Him in return, and finally love all the people who come into our lives.

God's love has been poured out in our hearts
through the Holy Spirit Who has been given
to us.   ROMANS 5:5

Forgiven

Pardoned; remitted

There are many instances in the Old Testament of God's anger when His people, the Israelites, would complain, disobey, and worship idols and false gods. But the amazing thing is how quickly God completely forgave them—He restored all of His benefits to them as soon as they turned back to Him.

Perhaps today you feel that God is angry with you. He is not! God is ready and willing to forgive your sins. He understands your weaknesses. He knows that we all, at times, succumb to temptations and wrong behavior, but He is a compassionate, loving

Father who has provided for our forgiveness in Christ. All we need to do is ask and receive!

The very fact that we cannot do everything right is why God sent Jesus to pay the price for our redemption. God is not angry with you. Choose to accept and walk in His forgiveness today!

*To the Lord our God belong mercy and
loving-kindness and forgiveness.*

DANIEL 9:9

Perfect

Finished; complete; consummate; not defective; having all that is requisite to its nature and kind

---

There are many things in life that I don't know, and so much about God that I am still learning, but I do know that I love God as much as I possibly can at this point in my spiritual journey.

Although I don't believe we can have a perfect performance in our walk with God, I do believe that we can have a perfect heart toward Him by loving Him wholeheartedly, desiring to please Him and living in a way that brings Him glory.

A person with a perfect heart toward

God always wants to grow, so keep growing in God and enjoy fellowship with Him today and every day.

Be perfect [growing into complete maturity of godliness in mind and character, having reached the proper height of virtue and integrity], as your heavenly Father is perfect.

MATTHEW 5:48

Believe

To expect or hope with confidence; to trust

If we continually try to earn God's approval by our own deeds, we will always have something separating us from Him. But if we come to Him by faith alone, trusting in His goodness, then we find an open-door policy and the freedom to enter at any time. You might say the password into God's presence is "believe."

I keep a sign sitting on a table in my office that says, in big, bold letters, BELIEVE. I do it to remind myself that is what God wants from me. He wants me to trust Him, place my faith in Him, and believe His Word. And when we whole-heartedly believe, it leads us to obedience.

I want to encourage you today to run to God, not away from Him. He has every-thing you need and offers it freely if you will simply come to Him and believe.

And [so that you can know and understand]
what is the immeasurable and unlimited and
surpassing greatness of His power in and for us
who believe, as demonstrated in the working
of His mighty strength.   EPHESIANS 1:19

Grace

Favor; mercy; pardon

We cannot earn God's approval. So then how can we get it? Receiving God's grace that is provided in Jesus is the answer to this problem. We must know that it is not anything we do, but God's amazing grace that invites us into a loving relationship with Him.

Grace is a gift that can't be purchased with our performance or anything else—it can only be received by faith.

Grace is God's undeserved favor! It is His love, mercy, and forgiveness available at no cost to us. Grace is also the power to change us and make us into what He wants us to be. There is no limit to God's grace, and it is available to restore and lift us up anytime we fail.

You can be free today from the anger and anxiety caused by perfectionism by giving up your own works and trusting in the work that Jesus has done for us all. Remember, God simply requires you to believe in the One Whom He has sent (John 6:28–29).

For the law was given through Moses; grace and truth came through Jesus Christ.

JOHN 1:17 (NIV)

Preserve

To uphold; to sustain

It is a good thing to help others and should be a major part of our life, but in the quest to help others, many people routinely ignore their own basic needs. Eventually they become bitter and turn into martyrs who feel they are being taken advantage of.

Once the body breaks down and life is no longer joyful, it becomes increasingly hard to serve anyone. Volunteers in a soup kitchen don't let their pots fall apart while they ladle out one more bowl of soup. They take the time to care for the equipment they need to do their calling. And you can do the same with your most important piece of equipment—your body.

We need balance in all things and that includes the area of helping others and taking care of ourselves. You are not being selfish if you take time and finances to take care of yourself; you are being wise. We are called to live sacrificially and be involved in doing good works, but let's not ignore our own basic needs in the process.

Beloved, I pray that you may prosper in every way and [that your body] may keep well.

3 JOHN 2

Relationship

**The state of being related by
kindred, affinity, or other alliance**

Religion is far different than relationship—
and far less than God's best. A religious
attitude is one of the worst that anyone
can have.

Jesus said that religious people can easily tell others what to do, but they don't
always do it themselves. They also place
heavy burdens on others by demanding
that they perform perfectly, but then they
won't even lift a finger to help. When they
do good works, they do them in order to be
seen, so even their motives for doing them
are self-serving (see Matthew 23:1–5).

In order to avoid a religious attitude and live in relationship with God, we can pray for God to reveal the beauty of intimacy with Him and true righteousness to us. Don't ever be satisfied with a phony copy of the real thing Jesus died to give you. Choose to love God and receive His love—choose relationship with Him.

For your Maker is your Husband—the Lord of hosts is His name—and the Holy One of Israel is your Redeemer; the God of the whole earth He is called.   ISAIAH 54:5

Respond

To answer; to reply

No matter how carefully you plan your progress in life, you will have setbacks. That's part of the process. One of the big differences between successful and unsuccessful people is not whether they have setbacks or even the frequency of their setbacks but how they respond to them.

Successful people are able to fall and get right back up again.

Having a bad day does not mean you have to have a bad life. Instead of focusing on a setback, consider keeping a journal of all your little successes, and thank God for each one. When you have a discouraging day or one where you feel you've done everything wrong, read your journal. You may be amazed at how far you've come.

Roll your works upon the Lord [commit and trust them wholly to Him; He will cause your thoughts to become agreeable to His will, and] so shall your plans be established and succeed.   PROVERBS 16:3

Decide

**To determine; to form a definite
opinion; to come to a conclusion**

We often assume that we are not responsible for what goes through our minds and
there is simply nothing we can do about it,
but that is not true.

God's Word gives us clear instructions
concerning what to think about and what
not to think about. It also teaches us that
we have the ability to decide to keep the
good thoughts and cast out the thoughts
that poison our lives. We are instructed to
cast down wrong imaginations and lead
them away captive to the obedience of
Jesus Christ.

God has wonderful plans for our lives, but in order to enjoy those plans we must live in agreement with Him, and it begins in our thinking (see Romans 12:2). We have the opportunity to think as God thinks in order to have what God wants us to have, to do what God wants us to do, and to be who He wants us to be.

We lead every thought and purpose away captive into the obedience of Christ.

2 CORINTHIANS 10:5

Greater

Chief; of vast power and excellence; supreme; illustrious; as the great God; the great Creator

---

Many times, before your feet even hit the floor in the mornings, the enemy begins to remind you of everything you did wrong the previous day or everything that didn't work out well. In doing so, the enemy's goal is to use yesterday to keep you from living today.

You don't have to be afraid of repeating the past. If you believe God is greater than your sins, mistakes, and shortcomings, you will have the spiritual energy and the strength and the grace of God to help you press on and do better in the future. The dreams of your future have no room for the disappointments of the past. They will keep you stuck and weighed down.

Every day can be a new beginning if we make a determined decision to press on to achieve the greater things God has for us today. God's mercy is greater than yesterday's mistakes.

> *One thing I do [it is my one aspiration]: forgetting what lies behind and straining forward to what lies ahead, I press on.*
>
> PHILIPPIANS 3:13–14

Available

Having sufficient power, force, or efficacy, for the object; valid

---

Too often we allow ourselves to become overly concerned about our weaknesses. The truth is, you don't have to be worried about your weaknesses. God is not at all surprised by them because He knows everything there is to know about you.

God is not looking for *ability*; He's looking for *availability*.

I encourage you to wake up every day and say: "Here I am, God. Is there anything You want me to do? Do You have something new for me today? I'm going to be bold and courageous in You, Lord. I'm available for whatever You have planned for my life."

If you'll have this attitude, you'll be amazed at the ways God will use you to change the world around you.

Also I heard the voice of the Lord, saying,
Whom shall I send? And who will go for Us?
Then said I, Here am I; send me.

ISAIAH 6:8

Empowered

Authorized; having legal or moral right

Though you do have an enemy, I want to be very clear about this: You have nothing to fear. The devil has no power over you—none!

The moment you gave your life to the Lord, you became a redeemed, forgiven, righteous child of God. Satan has no rightful place in your life.

Rather than live in fear of your enemy, you are empowered by God to live a bold, confident, productive, happy life that overcomes the enemy at every turn. You don't ever have to live in worry or doubt, wondering, "Is the enemy going to defeat me today?"

The Spirit of God in you is greater than any attack of the devil. Don't be afraid of the enemy; be confident of the power of God in your life.

He Who lives in you is greater (mightier) than he who is in the world.   1 JOHN 4:4

Equipped

Furnished with habiliments, arms, and whatever is necessary for a military expedition, or for a voyage or cruise

---

One of the benefits of being a Christian is that you have been equipped by God to take a stand. You have power and authority in Jesus to stand your ground, to move forward, to win any battle. You have been given:

- The belt of truth (living in the truth of Scripture)
- The breastplate of righteousness (knowing you have right standing with God because of Jesus)

- The shoes of peace (walking in peace with God)
- The shield of faith (believing God's promises)
- The helmet of salvation (hope that accompanies your salvation)
- The sword of the Spirit (speaking God's Word)

Go through today with boldness and strength in Christ. You have been equipped with everything you need to overcome.

Be strong in the Lord and in the power of His might. Put on the whole armor of God.

EPHESIANS 6:10–11 (NKJV)

Action

Literally, a driving; hence, the state of acting or moving; exertion of power or force

---

Passivity is the opposite of action and it is very dangerous. A passive person would like to see something good happen, but they just sit where they are and wait to see if it does.

God wants His people to be active. He gives creative ideas, big dreams, and an aggressive, active attitude. God's only direction is forward. He wants us to be decisive, energized by His Spirit and enthusiastic about life. Pray regularly for energy, passion, zeal, and enthusiasm.

Passivity is a bad habit and it can take a lot to break free from it, but you can do it by God's grace. Don't let uncertainty, disappointments, or laziness keep you stuck in a rut. Ask God to help you actively pursue His great plan for your life.

But someone will say [to you then], You [say you] have faith, and I have [good] works. Now you show me your [alleged] faith apart from any [good] works [if you can], and I by [good] works [of obedience] will show you my faith.   JAMES 2:18

Bigger

Great in spirit; lofty; brave

In order to embrace our purpose in life, it is important to dream, because dreams help stir our passion just as passion helps stir our dreams. It's important to think big when it comes to dreams for our future.

Too many of us don't think big enough, but I believe little thinkers will live little lives. People who cannot conceive of anything beyond what they can see with their natural eyes miss out on the best God has planned for them.

I recommend you think big thoughts, dream big dreams, and make big plans. We serve a big God who is able to do exceedingly, abundantly, above and beyond all we could ever hope, ask, or think (see Ephesians 3:20). Don't think of what you can or can't do in your own strength. Dare to think of what you can accomplish in God's strength.

But Jesus looked at them and said, With men this is impossible, but all things are possible with God.   MATTHEW 19:26

Choice

Care in selecting; judgment or skill in distinguishing what is to be preferred, and in giving a preference

---

Our imaginations and mind prepare us for action. They can prepare us for success or failure, joy or misery—the choice is up to us.

If you think about the past mistakes and all the things you have done wrong, it will only weaken you. It handicaps you as you try to enter the future God has for you. No matter what you have done in the past, learn to see yourself as a new creature in Christ (see 2 Corinthians 5:17). Choose to look forward in faith, not backward in guilt or condemnation.

In order to overcome shame, we can make the choice to stop thinking about our past failures. Rather than thinking about the sin, begin to praise God that you have been forgiven. See the solution, not the problem. When you do, you'll understand the joy of being a new creation in Christ!

Therefore, [there is] now no condemnation…
for those who are in Christ Jesus, who live [and]
walk not after the dictates of the flesh, but after
the dictates of the Spirit.   ROMANS 8:1

Blessing

Any means of happiness; a gift, benefit, or advantage

Just as we cannot earn salvation, we cannot earn any of the blessings of God. If we love God, we will strive to do what is right, not in order to get anything from Him, but because of what we have been given freely by His grace.

One of the best lessons we can learn is how to thankfully receive all that God wants to give. He desires to show His love for you in tangible ways. He will give you favor, open doors of opportunity for you, meet your needs, and bless you in amazing ways.

But if you cannot receive what He gives, you stop the process before it is completed. God is a giver, and we must receive from Him before we will have anything to give to others.

For out of His fullness (abundance) we have all received [all had a share and we were all supplied with] one grace after another and spiritual blessing upon spiritual blessing and even favor upon favor and gift [heaped] upon gift.   JOHN 1:16

Come

To draw nigh; to approach; to arrive; to be present

Any person can come to Christ. To do so requires no special talent. We just need to be ready to say we need help and then humble ourselves and come to God's throne of grace, receiving by faith the help and comfort that we need.

Jesus says in Matthew 11:29 that He is "gentle and humble in heart." He wants to make sure we understand His nature. He is a Helper who delights in lifting His people up.

When the prodigal son returned home in Luke 15, his father was delighted. He wasn't angry, and he didn't reject his son. Instead, he saw his son a long way off and ran to him. He was glad his son came home.

That's the way God feels about you. You can come to Him anytime—He's always glad when you do.

Come to Me, all you who labor and are heavy-laden and overburdened, and I will cause you to rest. [I will ease and relieve and refresh your souls.]   MATTHEW 11:28

Acceptance

A receiving with approbation or satisfaction; favorable reception

---

We were designed and created by God for acceptance and not for rejection. Because it is an inherent need in us, we crave it, and we need to live in an atmosphere of acceptance in order to grow and make progress.

What if we are rejected and unwanted by the people in our lives? Although it is painful, we can still choose to receive God's acceptance and know that He wants us. *God wants you! He accepts you!*

God is the giver of life, and He has created each of us carefully and purposely. No matter who rejects us, God accepts us.

And that is enough to enable us to be successful in life.

Jesus was despised and rejected by men, but He focused on God's love for Him. We can do the same thing—we can focus on God's unending love and acceptance for us.

> *For the Lord will not reject his people; he will*
> *never forsake his inheritance.*
>
> PSALM 94:14 (NIV)

Potential

Anything that may be possible

God created you with great potential to live for Him and make a difference in this world. Let me suggest that instead of focusing on what you can't do, what you didn't do, and what you don't do, focus on what you *can* do, what you *have* done, and what you *are* doing.

We absolutely must see ourselves, and our lives, in a positive way. Thinking too much about what you didn't do in the past and how things didn't work out the last time you tried will simply prevent you from trying again.

Make a purposeful decision to focus on at least one thing you have been successful at and that will energize you to try something else. In Christ, you do have potential, you are gifted, and you are capable of doing great things. You will be robbing the rest of us of your gifts, ideas, and talents if you won't believe it.

> *I have strength for all things in Christ Who empowers me [I am ready for anything and equal to anything through Him Who infuses inner strength into me; I am self-sufficient in Christ's sufficiency].*   PHILIPPIANS 4:13

Priority

Precedence in place or rank

We often get sidetracked simply because we want to be involved in everything that is going on. We don't want to miss anything. But the truth is we can't do everything. We must choose what is most important to us and focus on that.

To be able to focus means that we have to say no to many other things. Some of the things we say no to may be things we would like to say yes to. However, when we compare them to our main goals in life, we find we still need to say no. You cannot have everything you want and have anything worth having.

Making wise choices is the key to success. Choose to do now what you will be satisfied with later on. The only way to live without regrets is to do what you know you should do, when you know you should do it.

Roll your works upon the Lord [commit and trust them wholly to Him; He will cause your thoughts to become agreeable to His will, and] so shall your plans be established and succeed.   PROVERBS 16:3

Affirmation

The act of affirming or asserting as true; opposed to negation or denial

---

First thing when you wake up in the morning, before all the busyness of the day comes flying at you, take a moment with God and refresh your spirit with His strength. This will give you the mental and emotional peace that is the foundation of success. You can write an affirmation that addresses your specific needs, or you can use this one that I wrote:

"God, I am free by the power of Your Word. I believe You have given me the strength to break free from the bonds that have been

*holding me back from all the beautiful things
You have planned for me. I thank You that I
am free by the blood of Jesus and the sacrifice
that He made on the cross of Calvary. Thank
You for making me free through the truth
of Your Word and for empowering me with
Your power, strength, and wisdom. Help me
to be all You want me to be. In Jesus' name,
amen."*

*Sanctify them [purify, consecrate, separate
them for Yourself, make them holy] by the
Truth; Your Word is Truth.*   JOHN 17:17

Willpower

The trait of resolutely controlling your own behavior

We all know about willpower. Willpower is that thing that makes us dismiss the chocolate fudge sundae even though every cell of our bodies screams for us to dig in. Willpower is that thing CEOs and professional athletes tell us they use to trounce the competition.

Willpower and discipline are important and vitally necessary to a successful life, but willpower alone won't be enough. Determination gets you started and keeps you going—for a while. But it is never enough to bring you across the finish line.

What would happen if, instead of turning first to willpower in your time of need, you turned to God? God releases His power into your willpower and energizes it to bring you across the finish line. Jesus said in John 15:5, "Apart from Me...you can do nothing." This is one of the most important lessons we can learn if we want to enjoy the life Jesus died to give us.

"Not by might nor by power, but by My Spirit," says the Lord of hosts.

ZECHARIAH 4:6 (NKJV)

Go

**To walk; to move on the feet or
step by step**

Inaction is one of the main culprits that
keeps us from enjoying the life God has
for us. Inaction is like a heavy anchor that
holds you down. Fear, disbelief, worry,
and anxiety will do everything they can
to keep you stuck in the starting blocks
of inaction while others run their race all
around you.

You may not know where the finish line
is, and you may not know what will happen when you cross it, but—by the grace of
God—you know how to take a step. And
right now, that's all God is asking you to do.

Don't let the length of the journey intimidate you. Don't let the uncertainties of the terrain make you afraid. All you have to do is take the first step. And if you're feeling nervous or unsure, listen carefully. You just might hear a voice from heaven encouraging: Go...go...go! God's been cheering you on the whole time.

I [the Lord] will instruct you and teach you in the way you should go; I will counsel you with My eye upon you.   PSALM 32:8

Thankful

Grateful; impressed with a sense of kindness received, and ready to acknowledge it

---

If you've ever wondered, *What is God's will for my life?* the apostle Paul says in 1 Thessalonians that the first answer to that question is to be thankful.

One of the best ways to enjoy your life is to stop and thank God for the good things He has given you, no matter how big or small. Sometimes we are so anxious to get something new from God, we aren't enjoying the things He has already blessed us with.

When you aren't sure what step to take,

I encourage you to take the "thanksgiving step": Actively thank God for His kindness, His goodness, and His faithfulness in your life. You'll be amazed at how this action will change your perspective and affect your day.

> *Thank [God] in everything [no matter what the circumstances may be, be thankful and give thanks], for this is the will of God for you [who are] in Christ Jesus [the Revealer and Mediator of that will].*   1 THESSALONIANS 5:18

Learn

To gain knowledge

Many people today continue to fall back into the mistakes and patterns of their past. They keep going around the same mountain, time and time again, having to learn the same lesson multiple times.

Wisdom is learning from your mistakes and moving on. You don't have to keep making the same error or keep failing in the same area of life—you can have victory once and for all!

Let's say you lost your temper and yelled at your kids or your spouse yesterday. Well, that was a mistake. It's not God's best and you probably felt the conviction of the

Holy Spirit the moment it happened. You have a choice to make. You can: 1) *Be condemned for your mistake* 2) *Be glad you've been forgiven, but don't bother to learn anything,* or 3) *Take your mistake to God and ask Him to forgive you and teach you from it.* If you'll choose to learn from your mistakes, you'll begin growing in spiritual maturity, peace, and the joy of the Lord.

For [skillful and godly] wisdom will enter
your heart and knowledge will be pleasant to
your soul.   PROVERBS 2:10 (AMP)

Give

To bestow; to confer; to pass or transfer the title or property of a thing to another person without an equivalent or compensation

---

There are many people around us on a daily basis who are in need. People we could bless if we took a moment to think about how we could help them.

I have learned that true giving is not giving until I can feel it. Giving away clothes and household items that are old and I am finished with may be a nice gesture, but it does not equate to real giving. Real giving occurs when I give something

I want to keep, or I make an effort that will give aid to someone else.

That's how God gave to us. When He sent Jesus to pay for our sins, He gave His very best. God gave us His only Son because He loves us, so what will love cause us to do? Can we at least be inconvenienced or uncomfortable occasionally in order to help someone in need?

In everything I have pointed out to you [by example] that, by working diligently in this manner, we ought to assist the weak, being mindful of the words of the Lord Jesus, how He Himself said, It is more blessed (makes one happier and more to be envied) to give than to receive. ACTS 20:35

Timing

The time when something happens

The proper time for things is God's time, not ours. We are usually in a hurry, but God never is. We are often impatient and ready for everything to happen right now, but God, in His wisdom, prepares us first for what He wants to do in our lives, and preparation takes time.

God takes time to do things right—He lays a solid foundation before He attempts to build a building. We are God's building under construction. He is the Master Builder, and He knows what He is doing.

God's timing seems to be His own little secret. The Bible promises that He will never be late, but I have also discovered that He is usually not early. The good thing to know is that He is always right on time, and His timing is perfect.

And let us not lose heart and grow weary and
faint in acting nobly and doing right, for
in due time and at the appointed season we
shall reap, if we do not loosen and relax our
courage and faint. GALATIANS 6:9

Transformation

Metamorphosis; change of form in insects; as from a caterpillar to a butterfly

---

When we come to the point where we want to change or transform our lives, we can't do it alone. Only God can work in us, from the inside out, and that is real transformation.

For any change in behavior to last, it must come from the heart. We might be able to muster enough discipline to change *some* of our behavior, but only God can change our hearts.

God doesn't come barging into our lives; He waits to be invited to do the transforming work. Our responsibility is to want to change and to ask God to have His way in us. God's responsibility is to do the work while we believe, study His Word, spend time with Him, and cooperate with His instructions.

Do not be conformed to this world (this age), [fashioned after and adapted to its external, superficial customs], but be transformed (changed) by the [entire] renewal of your mind [by its new ideals and its new attitude].   ROMANS 12:2

Triumph

To obtain victory

The Bible says that when God gives your enemies over to you, then you must "utterly destroy" them (see Deuteronomy 7:1–2). But it's important to understand that we cannot triumph over and destroy spiritual enemies like anger, selfishness, bitterness, jealousy, and many others all at one time, or instantly.

God deals with things in our lives one at a time—and the changes we desire require patience. If you get ahead of God, you will get very frustrated and confused. Without God it is impossible to triumph even if we have the best of intentions.

Whatever spiritual enemy you are facing today, ask God to go before you and to give you the victory. Don't rush ahead, trying to do it in your own strength. Pray, listen, and wait on God. He will give you victory over any sin, bad habit, or addiction in your life.

But thanks be to God, Who in Christ always leads us in triumph [as trophies of Christ's victory] and through us spreads and makes evident the fragrance of the knowledge of God everywhere.   2 CORINTHIANS 2:14

Imperfect

Not finished; not complete

Much of the anguish over our flaws and weaknesses simply comes from trying to impress ourselves with our own perfection. We desperately want to feel good about ourselves, but we don't realize we can feel good about ourselves even when we make mistakes, especially when we are sorry for them and we want to improve.

God sees your heart! He is more interested in *you* than in your performance.

If you have children, you know you didn't get angry with them if they fell down while trying to learn to walk, or if they spilled food while trying to learn to feed themselves. You comforted them, encouraged them, cleaned them up, and helped them along the way.

God is the same way with us. He is not angry about our imperfections, and He wants to help us. Receive God's love and mercy and enjoy your journey.

My little children, these things I write to you, so that you may not sin. And if anyone sins, we have an Advocate with the Father, Jesus Christ the righteous.   1 JOHN 2:1 (NKJV)

Self-Image

One's own idea of oneself or sense of one's worth

Because self-image is so important, I want to share some truths for you to think about and speak over your life daily. As you do, they will help remold your image of yourself, and you can see yourself as God sees you.

- I know God created me, and He loves me unconditionally.
- I am not a failure just because I am not perfect.
- I have right standing with God through Jesus Christ.

- I like myself. I do not like everything I do, and I want to change—but I refuse to reject myself.
- God has a good plan for my life. I am going to fulfill my destiny and be all I can be for His glory.
- I am nothing, and yet I am everything. In myself I am nothing, and yet in Jesus, I am everything I need to be!

I will confess and praise You for You are fearful and wonderful and for the awful wonder of my birth!   PSALM 139:14

Exercise

Exertion of the body, as conducive to health; action; motion, by labor, walking, riding, or other exertion

---

Exercise has an astonishing effect on stress and depression, and it promotes all-around good health. I've read that a half hour of moderate exercise a day is as effective in relieving mild depression as some antidepressants. Doctors and dieticians agree: exercise is good for the body!

How does exercise do this? One way is by triggering the release of endorphins, chemicals in the brain that are responsible for good moods. Perhaps the brain does this to compensate for the sore muscles exercise can cause. No one knows for sure.

Whatever the reason, it is another one of God's ways to care for our bodies—and that's all we really need to know. If you're not making time each day to get some exercise, maybe it's time to reevaluate your schedule.

Your body is the temple (the very sanctuary) of the Holy Spirit Who lives within you.

1 CORINTHIANS 6:19

Ideal

**Existing in idea; intellectual;
mental; as ideal knowledge**

A great and practical way to improve your
life is to create a vision of the ideal you.
Carry this vision around in your thoughts
as you might carry a photo in your wallet. See yourself the way you want to be,
the way God says you can be, instead of
merely how you have always been

With God's help, say and do the things
the "ideal you" would do, instead of what
the "old you" would have done. If you
have never been a disciplined person but
ideally you would like to be one, start saying, "I am disciplined. I feel great, I take

care of myself, and I stay on task." Believe that God has given you discipline and self-control and start walking in it.

Make your goals concrete by writing them down. God told Habakkuk to write his vision down (Habakkuk 2:2) and we can follow his example.

The thoughts of the [steadily] diligent tend only to plenteousness, but everyone who is impatient and hasty hastens only to want.

PROVERBS 21:5

Mind-set

A fixed mental attitude or disposition that predetermines a person's responses to and interpretations of situations

---

The Bible teaches us that if we set our minds on the flesh, the flesh and its lusts and desires will control us. However, if we set our minds on the Spirit, we will be controlled by the Spirit. Many people don't realize that whatever we set our minds on is what we are seeking in life. What has your mind-set been lately?

Have you set your mind to pursue the purpose of God passionately, or are you pursuing your own plan and expecting

God to bless it? Sometimes the best thing we can do is throw away all of our own plans and say, "God, Your will be done in my life." When we do this, we step out into an adventure with God that gives us fresh passion. Don't be limited by your own thoughts and desires. God's plan is bigger and better!

For those who are according to the flesh and are controlled by its unholy desires set their minds on and pursue those things which gratify the flesh, but those who are according to the Spirit and are controlled by the desires of the Spirit set their minds on and seek those things which gratify the [Holy] Spirit.

ROMANS 8:5

Enthusiastically

With zeal

God wants us to be positive, joyful, and enthusiastic. There is nothing negative about God, and if we want to walk with Him and have His plans manifest themselves in our lives, it is essential that we choose to not be negative, too.

A positive attitude filled with hope fuels joy and enthusiasm. Your attitude is entirely yours. Nobody can make you have a good or bad one; it is entirely your choice.

Your decision determines the quality of your life. So why not make a decision to look on the bright side of life and let enthusiasm soar and take you to new heights in God's good plan.

Love one another... Never lag in zeal and in
earnest endeavor; be aglow and burning with
the Spirit, serving the Lord.

ROMANS 12:10–11

Simplify

To reduce what is complex; to make plain or easy

One of the best ways to battle stress and anxiety is to simplify your life. That may sound impossible to do but it really isn't, because God gives us wisdom in His Word to do it. Seek God first, and you'll be encouraged by the practical direction He reveals as you do so.

Here are a few ways in which you can use a simple approach to life:

- When a problem arises believe the best instead of the worst.

- Don't buy more than you can comfortably pay for.
- If your schedule is overcrowded, then cut out the nonessential things.
- If you're tired every morning, change your evening schedule so that you get to bed earlier.

It all sounds simple, but that's the point. The simple approach to facing your problems leaves room for joy in the midst of them, and they get solved much quicker.

But seek first the kingdom of God and His righteousness, and all these things shall be added to you.   MATTHEW 6:33 (NKJV)

Cheer

To dispel gloom, sorrow, silence, or apathy; to cause to rejoice; to gladden; to make cheerful

---

Difficulty is never enjoyable, but right thinking in the midst of it will cheer us up. Even though we have trials, we can face them with courage, being confident of God's love and His promise to help us. It seems to me that joy and happiness come more from what we believe than from what is happening to us.

Would you be willing to make some changes in your approach to life and even develop some new habits if it would enable you to have more joy and enjoyment?

Perhaps if we studied the habits and attitudes of happy people, we would be able to see some of the things we might need to change if we truly want to be happy. If we value joy, then we cannot just passively sit and wish to be happy; we can aggressively pursue it and be willing to make adjustments where they are needed.

A glad heart makes a cheerful countenance,
but by sorrow of heart the spirit is broken.

PROVERBS 15:13

Sword

An offensive weapon worn at the side and used by hand either for thrusting or for cutting

---

God has given us the weapons we need to win every battle we face. God's Word is a sharp sword for us, and we can wield it against the enemy.

Our swords will not do any good if we keep them in their sheaths, just as a Bible won't help us if it just sits on a shelf gathering dust. Our swords will be effective only if we use them. As we study, believe, and speak the Word of God, we're using "the sword that the Spirit wields."

If you wake up one morning feeling

discouraged and defeated, fight against the enemy of your soul by saying, "I will not give up! God has plans to give me a future and a hope and I am going to keep trusting God, so I can experience them" (see Jeremiah 29:11).

Use the Word of God to defeat every tactic of the devil. The Word of God is a powerful weapon that will not fail.

And take the helmet of salvation and the swordthat the Spirit wields, which is the Word of God.   EPHESIANS 6:17

Through

From end to end, or from side to side; from one surface or limit to the opposite

---

We all go through difficult things in life, and oftentimes they are the very circumstances, challenges, and situations that help us become people who know how to overcome adversity.

We do not grow or become strong during life's good times; we grow when we press through difficulties without giving up.

Many times we think the phrase "I'm going through something" is bad news, but if we view it properly, we realize *going through* is good; it means we are not stuck!

We may be facing adversity, but at least we are moving forward.

When you pass through the waters, I will be with you, and through the rivers, they will not overwhelm you. When you walk through the fire, you will not be burned or scorched, nor will the flame kindle upon you.

ISAIAH 43:2

Excellence

A valuable quality; anything highly laudable, meritorious, or virtuous in persons, or valuable and esteemed in things

———————

Think about what would happen if all of us woke up each day and decided that whatever we did, we would do it with excellence. We would give it our all and do our best with nothing less than a hundred percent.

Would it change our impact? Would it change our relationships? Would it change the world? I believe it would!

Doing things with excellence means you don't take shortcuts. You don't take the easy way just for the sake of its being easy. Instead, whatever you're doing, you give it your very best effort.

Make a decision to be an excellent person today. Slow down, think seriously about what you are doing, and ask yourself if you're doing it with your whole heart, and doing your very best.

Then this Daniel distinguished himself
above the governors and satraps, because an
excellent spirit was in him; and the king gave
thought to setting him over the whole realm.

DANIEL 6:3 (NKJV)

Discipline

Instruction and government, comprehending the communication of knowledge and the regulation of practice

---

Successful people are always disciplined, and undisciplined people are always unsuccessful. Success does not just fall on people; they must be disciplined, dedicated, and committed.

Are you a person of purpose, or do you just get up every day and wait to see how you feel before you make any plans? Are you easily swayed by what others want to do, or do you have a plan and are you disciplined enough to stick to your plan?

Mark Twain said the secret of success is to be able to make your vocation your vacation. I like that thought. It is not hard to be dedicated to what you love. When you love something and you're passionate about it, discipline comes easily.

And he must be hospitable [to believers, as well as strangers], a lover of what is good, sensible (upright), fair, devout, self-disciplined.   TITUS 1:8 (AMP)

Refresh

To give new strength to; to invigorate; to relieve after fatigue

---

Whenever we're stressed by the demands of life, the best thing we can do is go to God in prayer. Prayer is simply talking to God. Some people find time with God in the morning or evening to be the best method for nurturing calm and focus, but you can try it in mini-bursts, too.

Any time things start to feel overwhelming at work (or anywhere else, for that matter), take a few moments, breathe deeply, let your body relax, and ask God to refresh you.

Be very deliberate about it. Don't let

your mind race through one situation after another. With God's help, you'll feel your system calming down, and you'll be ready to return to your duties, prepared to do them with much greater clarity than you did previously.

He refreshes and restores my life (my self);
He leads me in the paths of righteousness
[uprightness and right standing with Him—
not for my earning it, but] for His name's
sake.   PSALM 23:3

Humility

In ethics, freedom from pride and arrogance; humbleness of mind; a modest estimate of one's own worth

---

In 1 Corinthians 15:10 the apostle Paul wrote, "But by the grace (the unmerited favor and blessing) of God I am what I am." If we do not realize that we are what we are by the grace of God, then we will think more highly of ourselves than we should.

Proud people compare themselves to others and feel superior if they are able to do something others cannot do. As Christians, we are to judge ourselves soberly (see Romans 12:3), knowing that without God, we cannot do anything of value and whatever we are able to accomplish is only by His grace. This knowledge is the key to living a humble life.

God gives us a measure of His own faith to do whatever He assigns us in life. He gives us abilities by His grace and favor, not by our own efforts.

> *But He gives more grace. Therefore He says: "God resists the proud, but gives grace to the humble."*   JAMES 4:6(NKJV)

Brand-new

Quite new; bright as a brand of fire

Regardless of any past failure or present struggle, God always offers a new beginning. Fresh starts aren't the exception; they're the rule. We see them all throughout the Word of God. For example:

- Far from his full potential, wandering on the back side of the desert, Moses is called to lead a nation. *Fresh start!*
- A victim of her reputation, known only as the harlot, Rahab is rescued and given a noble name in the lineage of Christ. *Fresh start!*

- Stuck in a dead-end job, tending sheep, David is anointed the next king of Israel. *Fresh start!*
- Widowed, alone, and with nowhere to go, Ruth is given a brand-new, better-than-imagined life. *Fresh start!*

The circumstances change, and the stories vary, but the grace of God never wavers. God always offers a new chance. A new opportunity. A new life.

Behold, I am doing a new thing! Now it springs forth.   ISAIAH 43:19

Positive

Opposed to negative, as positive good

Oftentimes the negativity of others can wear off on us. But the truth is you don't have to sit around and listen to friends or co-workers murmur and complain all day. If you stay in that environment, it is going to affect your spirit. You may not be able to avoid them every second of the day, but you can limit the access they have to you.

Maybe you need to listen to part of a good teaching during your break. Or maybe you need to take a walk and seek fellowship with God during your lunch rather than join a negative conversation.

The most important thing is to realize that positive, faith-filled words will build your spirit up, but negative words will tear it down. Don't allow the negativity of those around you to pull you down and take your focus away from the Lord. Fill your life with positive things that build you up and increase your joy.

Let no corrupt word proceed out of your mouth, but what is good for necessary edification, that it may impart grace to the hearers. EPHESIANS 4:29 (NKJV)

Expectation

The act of expecting or looking forward to a future event with at least some reason to believe the event will happen

---

One of the most important things you can do in life is let go of your need to please people or meet their expectations.

Trying to please others and meet their expectations will cause you to live the life *they* want you to live and to miss the life that God wants you to live. There is no joy in that, only bondage.

Rather than trying to please others, make it your aim to live your life in a way that pleases God. This is where you will find rest and peace for your soul. If you want to experience the life-changing joy of the Lord, let go of the unrealistic expectations of others and live for God.

Walk (live and conduct yourselves) in a
manner worthy of the Lord, fully pleasing
to Him and desiring to please Him in
all things.   COLOSSIANS 1:10

Secure

Certain; very confident

Insecurity is at epic proportions in our society. It seems we come across touchy, insecure people everywhere we go.

Insecurity keeps people so focused on their perceived weaknesses and what others think of them that they can't enjoy life. They live in fear and with a failure mentality because insecurity influences every decision they make.

As a child of God, you don't have to live under the storm clouds of insecurity; you can be secure in Christ as you live by faith, adhering to, relying on, and completely trusting in Him. When you choose to receive your acceptance and self-worth from God, you will never need to be insecure around people again. God wants you to live with a bold confidence, believing in faith that His plans and purposes will come to pass in your life.

I have been crucified with Christ [in Him I have shared His crucifixion]; it is no longer I who live, but Christ (the Messiah) lives in me; and the life I now live in the body I live by faith in (by adherence to and reliance on and complete trust in) the Son of God, Who loved me and gave Himself up for me.

GALATIANS 2:20

Faith

In theology, the assent of the mind or understanding to the truth of what God has revealed

---

God has good things in store for you, and you access them by putting your faith completely in Him. Fear is the opposite of faith, and it can keep you from the goodness of God in your life. But when fear knocks on the door, you can send faith to answer it. For example, when...

- Fear whispers, "You can't do this because you're too weak, inexperienced, hurt, or broken." Faith shouts, "I have strength for all things in Christ Who empowers me!" (Philippians 4:13).

- Fear whispers, "Why try? That's impossible for you to do." Faith shouts, "All things are possible with God!" (Matthew 19:26).

- Fear whispers, "You're not talented or smart enough." Faith shouts, "I am fearfully and wonderfully made!" (Psalm 139:14 NIV).

Believe by faith that all things are possible with God—He can do great things for you and through you!

So then faith comes by hearing, and hearing by the word of God.　　ROMANS 10:17 (NKJV)

Continue

To last; to be durable; to endure; to be permanent

One of the keys to success is to continue believing God. Even though we may not sense any change after we've prayed about something, it is vitally important that we continue believing in God's promise to deliver and help us.

When the Holy Spirit is walking me into freedom in any area, I often say that I am free from a thing even while I am still experiencing no freedom at all. By doing this, I am declaring my belief that God and His promise are greater than my problem and it is only a matter of time before I experience the fullness of His freedom.

Joy is released in our lives through believing. Once we choose to believe God's Word, we receive joy and peace, and that helps us enjoy life while we are waiting for the fullness of God's promises to manifest themselves.

The children of Your servants shall dwell safely and continue, and their descendants shall be established before You.

PSALM 102:28

Certain

Sure; true; undoubted; unquestionable; that cannot be denied; existing in fact and truth

---

While we all want a level of certainty about things in our lives, we live in a world full of uncertainty. Unless we keep our hope and expectation in God, the circumstances around us will create tremendous stress and anxiety. Certainty makes us feel safe, and we all desire that. We are safe with God, and through faith in Him we can relax in the midst of tumult.

Trusting God doesn't mean that everything turns out the way we want it to, but it does mean that it turns out the way that it should. God doesn't always lead us to the easy way in life. Sometimes we go through difficulties, but in the end God can use them for our good. Even when life hurts, God wants us to be certain of His love, provision, and goodness.

God is our hiding place and He wants us to feel safe as we journey through life.

So also, when you see these things happening, you may recognize and know that He is near, at [the very] door. MARK 13:29

Friendship

An attachment to a person, proceeding from intimate acquaintance, a reciprocation of kind offices, or from a favorable opinion of the amiable and respectable qualities of the person's mind

---

If we take time to get to know people well, we may like them more. There are lots of reasons why we decide too quickly that we don't like someone, but those are rarely valid reasons. We may make decisions about people based on what others have told us about them or a bad first impression.

Is there anyone you have decided you just don't like and have shut out of your life without ever really taking time to know them? That person you've been avoiding could be hurting and in need of your friendship or a listening ear. He or she could even be the friend you have been asking God to give you.

You will never know if you don't give them a chance.

Iron sharpens iron; so a man sharpens the countenance of his friend.   PROVERBS 27:17

Energy

Power exerted; vigorous operation; force; vigor

Fear, anger, doubt, guilt—these are just a few of the many emotions we dwell on that are wasted energy. You may feel these from time to time, but you don't have to hold on to them. Instead, you can use your energy to cast every care on God and live free from these wasted emotions. Here are a few ways to do that:

- If someone hurts your feelings or disappoints you, choose to forgive instead of getting angry.

- Don't waste your energy worrying, because it doesn't do any good anyway.
- When you sin, repent, receive your forgiveness, and be thankful that you don't have to live in guilt.
- If someone doesn't like you, pray for that person. The real problem may be that the person doesn't like him- or herself.

For this I labor [unto weariness], striving with all the superhuman energy which He so mightily enkindles and works within me.

COLOSSIANS 1:29

Practice

Frequent or customary actions; a succession of acts of a similar kind or in a like employment

---

We learn to trust God by actually doing it. As we step out in faith we receive grace to handle situations that are difficult or even seemingly impossible.

Sometimes our faith in God provides a deliverance from something difficult. At other times, we put our faith in God, and He gives us grace to "go through." We must leave the choice to Him, trusting that His ways are always best and will work out for our good. Each time we practice trusting God, it becomes easier to do so the next time.

If you are struggling with something right now in your life, ask yourself if you are putting your faith in God that His grace is sufficient to meet your need. Remember, grace is unmerited favor—it is God's power coming into your situation to do for you what you cannot do for yourself. Ask and receive that your joy may be full (John 16:24).

And they who know Your name [who have experience and acquaintance with Your mercy] will lean on and confidently put their trust in You, for You, Lord, have not forsaken those who seek (inquire of and for) You.

PSALM 9:10

Courageous

Brave; bold; daring; intrepid; hardy to encounter difficulties and dangers; adventurous; enterprising

---

As a believer, the only way you can lose in life is if you give up and stop moving forward. It's important to understand that courage isn't the absence of fear—courage is moving forward when you feel afraid. And when you do that, God will lead you straight through your fears and into His perfect will for your life.

You were not created to live a timid, shy, weak, fearful, boring life. Your destiny is to be bold, confident, and courageous—unafraid to try new things.

So instead of having an attitude that says, *I shouldn't try because I probably won't make it*, have an attitude that says, *I am going to step out with courage and not live in fear!* No matter what obstacle or challenges you face, you can press ahead because you have everything you need in Christ.

Be strong, vigorous, and very courageous. Be not afraid, neither be dismayed, for the Lord your God is with you wherever you go.

JOSHUA 1:9

Re-created

Refreshed; diverted; amused; gratified

Has there ever been a time in your life when you were so filled with fear or worry you just felt like giving up? Maybe there was a day or season when your frustration caused you to want to stop trying.

If so, I want to encourage you: You don't have to live in that despair. Instead you can live with confidence and assurance because Ephesians 2:10 says we have been "recreated in Christ Jesus, [born anew]." That means:

- Jesus is strong, so in Him, you have strength.

- Jesus is courageous, so in Him, you are fearless.
- Jesus is capable and confident, so in Him, you can do everything He has put in your heart to do.

Don't let fear or worry hold you back. Learn who you are in Christ and live the fulfilled life He offers as part of your inheritance from Him.

For we are God's [own] handiwork (His workmanship), recreated in Christ Jesus, [born anew].   EPHESIANS 2:10

Focus

A central point; point of concentration

Often called the former best woman soccer player in the world, Mia Hamm says she's often asked, "Mia, what's the most important thing for soccer players to have?" With no hesitation, she answers, "Mental toughness." She explains that when eleven players want to knock you down, when you're tired or injured, you can't let any of it affect your focus. "It is," says Hamm, "one of the most difficult aspects of soccer and the one I struggle with every game and every practice."

It is impossible to succeed at anything

without the power of focus. Whether you want to be a champion golfer, a champion mom, or a champion teacher, it is imperative that you learn to focus on the task at hand, and that means letting go of every other distraction.

We each want to be a champion at something. We want to be winners in life. We want to succeed. Focus is the tool that God gives us to help us be who we say we want to be and do what we say we want to do.

Looking...to Jesus, Who is the Leader and the Source of our faith...   HEBREWS 12:2

Unhurried

Relaxed and leisurely; without hurry or haste

The timing of God is never rushed or frantic. God is patient, and He causes things to happen according to His perfect, unhurried schedule for your life. The Israelites couldn't leave the bondage of Egypt until God's perfect time came. Joshua couldn't take Jericho until the exact right day. Jesus wasn't raised from the dead until the third day. These are examples of God's perfect timing.

Think of buying a five-thousand-piece puzzle. You buy it because you like the picture on the box, but when you dump out all the pieces on the table, you feel overwhelmed. All the things going on in our lives are a bit like that. We like the picture God presents in His Word of what we can become, but will we be patient enough to see the picture put together?

Never forget: God has a perfect way, a perfect plan, and a perfect time. All things work together in due time.

For the vision is yet for an appointed time and it hastens to the end [fulfillment]; it will not deceive or disappoint. Though it tarry, wait [earnestly] for it.   HABAKKUK 2:3

Aggressive

**Having or showing determination
and energetic pursuit of your ends**

Don't accept the lie that you are a timid
person, or that "fearful" is just your personality or the way you are. Some people
may be more naturally bold than others, but everyone can be effective and do
amazing things in their lives if they will
walk in faith and follow God.

It helps us to resist fear when we understand that Satan is the source of it. If we
believe it is just the way we are, then we
will accept it and sink into a low level of living that is not God's will. Godly aggression
is the key to effectiveness. We can't even be

effective in conquering daily chores if we don't attack them with an aggressive attitude.

Always lean on God and depend on His grace to make you victorious in your fight against fear. God is your deliverer! Know that God loves you, that He is for you, and that He is always with you.

And from the days of John the Baptist until the present time, the kingdom of heaven has endured violent assault, and violent men seize it by force [as a precious prize.] MATTHEW 11:12

Continually

**Without pause or cessation;
unceasingly**

How do you see yourself? Are you able to
honestly evaluate yourself and your behavior and not come under condemnation?
Are you able to look at how far you still
have to go but also look at how far you
have come?

Where you are now is not where you
will end up. If you are a born-again Christian, you are somewhere on the path of the
righteous. You may not be as far along as
you would like to be, but thank God you
are on the path.

Enjoy the glory you are in right now

and don't get jealous of where others may be. They had to pass through where you are at some time themselves.

And all of us, as with unveiled face, [because we] continued to behold [in the Word of God] as in a mirror the glory of the Lord, are constantly being transfigured into His very own image in ever increasing splendor and from one degree of glory to another; [for this comes] from the Lord [Who is] the Spirit.

2 CORINTHIANS 3:18

Regardless

Not looking or attending to

I encourage you to say every day, *"God is working in me right now—He is changing me!"* Speak what the Word of God says, regardless of what you feel.

It seems that we incessantly talk about how we feel. When we do that, it is difficult for the Word of God to work in us effectively. We magnify our feelings about everything else and allow them to take the lead role in our lives.

It is important that we live by faith, regardless of our feelings. The enemy makes sure we frequently *feel* that we are an unredeemable mess or that God is not working in our lives. This is why we must stand on God's Word every day, regardless of how we feel.

> *When you received the message of God [which you heard] from us, you welcomed it not as the word of [mere] men, but as it truly is, the Word of God, which is effectually at work in you who believe [exercising its superhuman power in those who adhere to and trust in and rely on it].*　　1 THESSALONIANS 2:13

Satisfied

**Having the desires fully gratified;
made content**

A lot of our problems are often a result of
complaining when we could have been
praising or thanking God. Complaining
is certainly not God's will or purpose for
His people. The whole world seems to be
complaining about something, but each of
us can make the decision to set a different
and more positive example.

If you cannot change something, then
change the way you think about it, but
don't complain about it.

The next time you are tempted to complain, please remember it does no good at

all. It is a complete waste of time and says loudly and clearly to God that you are not at all satisfied with the way He is taking care of you.

If you'll be satisfied and begin to thank God right where you are, He will help you get where you need to be.

Who satisfies your mouth ... with good so that your youth, renewed, is like the eagle's [strong, overcoming, soaring]!   PSALM 103:5

Faithful

**Firmly adhering to duty; of true
fidelity; loyal; true to allegiance**

I have experienced the unfaithfulness of
people many times in my life, but at the
same time, I have experienced the faithfulness of God. Indeed, God is not like
people!

God promises that He will never leave
you nor forsake you, but He will be with
you until the very end (see Matthew
28:20). He is with you in your times of
need, and He is planning to provide for
all your needs (see Hebrews 13:5). God is
with you when you are going through trials, and He is planning your breakthrough

(see 1 Corinthians 10:13). When all others forsake you, God will stand by you (see 2 Timothy 4:16–17).

Others may have hurt you or abandoned you, but God never will. He is ever faithful!

Yet the Lord is faithful, and He will strengthen [you] and set you on a firm foundation and guard you from the evil [one]. 2 THESSALONIANS 3:3

Covenant

A mutual consent or agreement of two or more persons

Under the old covenant, our sin could be covered by the sacrifices of animals, but never removed. The sense of guilt connected to sin was always present.

But the good news is that God has made a new covenant with man. It is a better covenant—far superior to the old. The old covenant was initiated with the blood of animals, but the new was initiated with the sinless blood of Jesus Christ.

Jesus took the punishment that we deserved, and promised that if we would believe in Him and all that He did for us,

He would forever stand in our place, and our responsibility to keep the law would be met in Him. The old covenant focused on what man could do, but the new covenant focuses on what God has done for us in Jesus Christ (see Romans 5).

This is the agreement (testament, covenant) that I will set up and conclude with them after those days, says the Lord: I will imprint My laws upon their hearts, and I will inscribe them on their minds (on their inmost thoughts and understanding).   HEBREWS 10:16

Good

**Useful; valuable; having qualities
or a tendency to produce a
beneficial effect**

God is good, without respect to persons.
In other words, He is good to all, all the
time. His goodness radiates from Him.

Not everything in our life is good, but
God can work it out for good if we will
trust Him. Joseph suffered much abuse at
the hands of his brothers as a young boy,
but later in life when he had an opportunity to get revenge against them, he said:
"You thought evil against me, but God
meant it for good" (Genesis 50:20). Joseph

could have been bitter, but he searched for the good in his painful situation.

God's entire motive and purpose is to do good to everyone who will receive it from Him. It is impossible for God not to be good, because it is His character. Don't think that God is like people, because His ways and thoughts are far above ours (see Isaiah 55:8–9).

How much more will your Father Who is in heaven [perfect as He is] give good and advantageous things to those who keep on asking Him!   MATTHEW 7:11

Please

To satisfy; to make content

Some people are addicted to approval. They cannot feel peaceful unless they believe everyone is pleased with them, and that is something that is next to impossible to accomplish.

We can't please people all the time, and it is vanity to try. But the one thing we can do is to make it our aim to please God. After all, His opinion is the only one that really matters.

I want to encourage you to be a God-pleaser, not a people-pleaser. When we live our lives to please others, we become weary and lose our peace and joy. However, the exact opposite is true when we live to please God. When we live for Him, our lives are filled with His peace, joy, and confidence.

Therefore, whether we are at home [on earth away from Him] or away from home [and with Him], we are constantly ambitious and strive earnestly to be pleasing to Him.

2 CORINTHIANS 5:9

Pathway

Usually, a narrow way to be passed on foot

The pathway to God is not perfect performance. Some people in a crowd asked Jesus what they needed to do to please God, and the answer Jesus gave was, "Believe in the One Whom He has sent" (see John 6:28–29).

That is so simple we can miss it. We need to believe in Jesus? That's it? Surely God wants more from us than that!

More than anything, God wants us to trust Him and to believe His Word. You can get off the treadmill of trying to be perfect, because you cannot buy or earn

God's love or His favor, not even with a perfect performance. It simply is not for sale.

For God so greatly loved and dearly prized the world that He [even] gave up His only begotten (unique) Son, so that whoever believes in (trusts in, clings to, relies on) Him shall not perish (come to destruction, be lost) but have eternal (everlasting) life.

JOHN 3:16

Rest

Cessation of motion or action of any kind, and applicable to any body or being

---

We have a desire to rest, not just physically but spiritually, mentally, and emotionally. We have a deep need and desire to enter what Scripture calls "the rest of God."

Jesus said that if we come to Him, He will give us rest for our souls (see Matthew 11:28). Hebrews 4:3 teaches us that we can enter the rest of God if we believe.

We want to rest from agonizing fears and frustrations, thoughts of doubt and insecurity, and our own striving to please God with our own efforts. Let us make a decision to believe God's Word, and the moment we do, then and only then can we rest from the weariness of our own works.

God loves you, He forgives you, and He is pleased with you because you are His child. Rest in that truth today.

So then, there is still awaiting a full and complete Sabbath-rest reserved for the [true] people of God   HEBREWS 4:9

Witness

Testimony; attestation of a fact or event

I once heard a story of a Christian man who prayed each morning: "Lord, if You want me to witness to someone today, please give me a sign to show me who it is."

One day he found himself on a bus and a big, burly man sat next to him. The big guy burst into tears and began to weep. He then cried out with a loud voice, "I need to be saved. I'm a sinner, and I need the Lord. Won't someone help me?"

He then turned to the Christian and pleaded, "Can you show me how to be saved?" The believer immediately bowed his head and prayed, "Lord, is this a sign?"

It's a humorous story, but the truth is God has called us to share our faith with others in the hopes of leading them to a relationship with Christ. It's not hard or something to be afraid of. Just be a witness—when God opens the door of opportunity, share what He has done for you and how He can do the same thing for them.

For I am not ashamed of the Gospel (good news) of Christ, for it is God's power working unto salvation. ROMANS 1:16

Decisive

Having the power or quality of determining a question, doubt, or any subject of deliberation; final; conclusive

---

In America we like options, but we have become so excessive that it has gotten confusing. We have so many clothes that we stand in our closet for long periods feeling that we have nothing to wear. We go to restaurants with a massive menu and cannot decide what to eat. Our large variety of choices has become a hindrance instead of a help to us.

I think we may have to aggressively practice just making a decision instead of wasting too much time trying to make one and possibly never doing so. We can focus on a few choices and then decide.

You might think, *What if I miss the best one?* But you can spend another hour trying to decide and still end up with the choice you made. Once we use our time, whether wisely or unwisely, it is gone forever. I think it is best not to waste it!

If any of you lacks wisdom, let him ask of God . . . and it will be given to him.

JAMES 1:5 (NKJV)

Suddenly

Without premeditation

It is important that we live with expectancy. We can expect things to change at any time instead of expecting them to always stay the way they have always been.

We can be encouraged to know that God can bring "suddenly moments" into our lives—moments that are so powerful and so miraculous, they change everything. One word from God, one touch from His Spirit, one promise from His Word, being in the right place at the right time, can set your life on a new course. Things can change in your life in a moment, suddenly!

Living with a positive expectancy is a facet of faith, and God's Word says that without faith, it is impossible to please God (Hebrews 11:6). It pleases God when we expect His divine help rather than expecting trouble. A good question to ask yourself is "What am I expecting?"

My soul, wait only upon God and silently submit to Him; for my hope and expectation are from Him. PSALM 62:5

Release

To free from obligation or penalty

Do you know what God does with the sins and mistakes of your past? He forgets them! Hebrews 8:12 says that God remembers your sins no more. His forgiveness is a free gift, and it is available all the time. I urge you to stop remembering what God has forgotten—release it.

No matter how hard you try, you are going to make mistakes; we all do. Mistakes are a part of life. How you respond to those mistakes is important in order for you to begin again. That doesn't mean you don't try to make right decisions and honor God with every part of your life; it just means you don't dwell on everything you did that was wrong.

Refuse to spend your days focused on your mistakes. Don't sit around thinking and talking about past failures. Release them and receive God's forgiveness.

Be gentle and forbearing with one another and, if one has a difference (a grievance or complaint) against another, readily pardoning each other; even as the Lord has [freely] forgiven you, so must you also [forgive].

COLOSSIANS 3:13

Strategy

An elaborate and systematic plan of action

_____

God is always giving His people new strategies. In 2 Samuel 5, God instructed David to attack the Philistines directly; David obeyed and the Israelites won a great victory. But the next time the Philistines attacked, God gave David a completely different strategy. David couldn't rely on an old plan—he had to trust God for something new.

I believe God wants you to trust Him for a new battle strategy. If you're frustrated today because the old methods aren't working in your marriage, your family, your finances, your career, or your ministry, do what David did—ask God to give you a new plan.

It's great to draw strength from past victories, but God wants you to draw close to Him, believing for the fresh, new thing He wants to do in the present.

Behold, the former things have come to pass,
and new things I now declare.   ISAIAH 42:9

Unafraid

Free from fear or doubt; easy in mind

Fear is what you pass on the way to success. I always say that most people fail but they can fail their way to success. In other words, it is impossible to ever find out what God has for your life without making a few mistakes along the way.

Don't be so addicted to your own perfection that you live a small life with no passion for much of anything because you've chosen to play it safe. You don't have to be flawless to enjoy life—you can learn, grow, and mature from each mistake.

Safe usually means sameness, but God

has created us for diversity and growth. He wants us to face new challenges, try new things, experiment, and be creative. The next time you are tempted to shrink back in fear, ask God to give you the courage to keep moving forward regardless of the fear.

Be strong, courageous, and firm; fear not nor be in terror before them, for it is the Lord your God Who goes with you.

DEUTERONOMY 31:6

Different

Distinct; separate; not the same as

Sometimes we settle for a mediocre life, doing things the way everyone around us does them, because we aren't bold enough to be the unique individuals God created us to be. For example, if you don't like your job, you hate the atmosphere at work (or at home), and you dread spending time there every day, ask yourself if you're doing anything to change the situation. You don't have to be like everyone else—you can be different. And you can be a difference maker!

Do you smile at everyone when you arrive, or do you frown like everyone else?

Have you said anything encouraging to your co-workers or your family today?

Why not think differently? Why not change the way you talk about your life and all of its aspects? I heard a song once titled, "I Love My Life," and I thought, *That is a great song I wish everyone were singing.*

If you'll change your outlook and your actions—if you'll decide to be different—you'll be amazed at the changes that will take place in yourself and in others.

Come out from among them and be separate, says the Lord.   2 CORINTHIANS 6:17 (NKJV)

Fresh

Recently from the well or spring; pure and cool; not warm or vapid

---

One of the fastest ways to stagnate is to find something wrong with everything and everybody, including yourself. On the other hand, thankful people are usually positive, happy people who look for the good in life.

One of the ways to be continually filled with the Spirit is to be thankful in everything (see 1 Thessalonians 5:18).

Thank God for your life, your job, your family, and your friends. Thank God you are breathing and that all things are possible with Him.

God never changes, but everything else is subject to change. You are not at a dead end; you are not stuck in a place you cannot escape. God has something fresh and new for you. Today is the beginning of the rest of your wonderful life, and you can make a decision that you are going to enjoy it.

To the end that my tongue and my heart and everything glorious within me may sing praise to You and not be silent. O Lord my God, I will give thanks to You forever.

PSALM 30:12

Everything

Whatever pertains to the subject under consideration

I encourage you to talk with God about absolutely everything. You can tell Him how you feel, what you desire and what your goals are. Tell Him what you love about Him and about your life, and express your gratitude for all that He has done for you.

You can tell God about the things in your life that you don't like or that are hard for you. Tell Him what you have done that is wrong, and talk with Him about all your concerns for yourself, your life, and your loved ones.

You can tell God absolutely anything, and He is never shocked or surprised because He knew all about it before it ever happened.

Pray at all times (on every occasion, in every season) in the Spirit, with all [manner of] prayer and entreaty. To that end keep alert and watch with strong purpose and perseverance, interceding in behalf of all the saints (God's consecrated people).

EPHESIANS 6:18

Well-Being

Welfare; happiness; prosperity

Good relationships are built on trust, and God wants us to choose to trust Him with ourselves and everything else in our lives.

God is faithful and it is impossible for Him to fail us. If something doesn't turn out the way would like it to, it may be because He has something better in mind for us and we simply don't know how to ask for it yet. God only has our benefit and well-being in His plan for us, and the best policy is always to relax and trust Him.

Waiting on God's timing is usually challenging for most of us, but His timing is always perfect. Things will turn out

better with God's plan than they would
with ours!

> *Therefore do not worry and be anxious,*
> *saying, What are we going to have to eat?*
> *or, What are we going to have to drink? or,*
> *What are we going to have to wear?... Your*
> *heavenly Father knows well that you need*
> *them all.*   MATTHEW 6:31–32

Compassion

A suffering with another; painful sympathy

God is compassionate and since we have His nature, we also have compassion. However, when we see others in need, it is possible to fail to operate in the compassion we have by ignoring their needs and suffering.

Jesus was moved with compassion (see Mark 1:41). He took action and relieved suffering, and we need to do the same thing. The first thing we can do when we see someone hurting is to pray for him or her. The next thing to do is ask God if there is anything we can do to help. A kind word, a smile, or lending a helping hand can encourage a hurting person and give them the needed strength to press on.

But if anyone has this world's goods (resources for sustaining life) and sees his brother and fellow believer in need, yet closes his heart of compassion against him, how can the love of God live and remain in him?   I JOHN 3:17

Righteous

Just; accordant to the divine law; denotes one who is holy in heart, and observant of the divine commands in practice

---

God views us as being right with Him through Jesus Christ. He sees us and thinks of us as being in Christ, and we can learn to do the same thing.

In ourselves, we are nothing of any value, and we can do very little right, but in Christ, we are amazing people who have been re-created in Christ Jesus. Because of Jesus, our standing before God is right and pure.

We are born anew that we may do

the good works that He has prearranged and made ready for us, that we may live the good life Jesus died for us to have (see Ephesians 2:10). God wants us to see ourselves the way He does. He wants us to understand that in Christ we are righteous in His sight.

May you abound in and be filled with the fruits of righteousness (of right standing with God and right doing) which come through Jesus Christ (the Anointed One).

PHILIPPIANS 1:11

Identify

To make to be the same

Are you kind to yourself? Do you say nice things about yourself, or are you more inclined to meditate on all of your faults? If we want to walk with God, we need to learn to think the way God thinks and know who we are in Christ. Here are some things God says about you in His Word:

- You are a new creature in Christ, old things have passed away and all things are made new (2 Corinthians 5:17).
- Jesus became sin for you and has made you the righteousness

of God in Him (2 Corinthians 5:21).

- God has handpicked you. He has chosen you to be His own in Christ because He loves you (Ephesians 1:4–5).
- You have gifts, talents, and abilities (Romans 12:5–6).
- God has a good plan for your future (Jeremiah 29:11).
- You are the home of God (1 Corinthians 3:16).

So God created man in His own image.

GENESIS 1:27

Overcome

To conquer; to vanquish; to subdue

When David defeated Goliath in 1 Samuel 17, he gave us a great example of what it means to have God on your side. You see, your problem may be bigger than you are, but it's not bigger than God.

If you had to face it on your own, you'd be in trouble, but you don't have to face it on your own. God is for you, and He can overcome any enemy or obstacle that threatens to hurt you.

I realize you may not have seen this problem coming, but God did. He is not surprised or intimidated by oversized obstacles—He's defeated giants before, and He can do it again.

Defeating giants is God's specialty. What looks like an obstacle can actually be an opportunity for you to overcome the enemy through Christ. Don't be afraid of the pressure. Stand strong in faith and watch the giants fall.

In the world you have tribulation and trials and distress and frustration; but be of good cheer [take courage; be confident, certain, undaunted]! For I have overcome the world.

JOHN 16:33

Led

**An obsequious follower or
attendant**

For many people, their security, peace, and
joy are connected to their circumstances.
If things are going well, they feel loved,
but if they are not going well, then they
think God doesn't love them or that they
are being punished for some sin they committed.

We are called to be led by the Word of
God and the Spirit, especially concerning
our thought life. We are not to be led by
our soul (mind, will, and emotions). We
may not be able to control what thoughts
pop into our minds or what feelings arise

in our hearts, but we can control what we *do* with those thoughts or feelings. We can be led by the Holy Spirit.

We don't have to let negative, destructive feelings rule our lives; instead, we can take authority over our emotions, submit them to God, and choose to stand on the Word of God.

> *Whatever things are pure, whatever things are lovely, whatever things are of good report, if there is any virtue and if there is anything praiseworthy—meditate on these things.*
>
> PHILIPPIANS 4:8 (NKJV)

Relate

To ally by connection or kindred

The Bible is the infallible, perfect Word of God, but it is full of examples of fallible, imperfect people that we can relate to. They are recorded in the Bible to encourage us to trust that God is faithful to us and He has equipped us to do whatever He's calling us to do in our lives.

For example: David got discouraged. Moses lacked confidence. Elijah got depressed. Gideon was afraid. Sarah laughed in disbelief at God's promise. The Israelites rebelled.

Isn't it encouraging to know that the men and women in the Bible weren't all like superheroes? They were real people with real problems just like you and me.

The next time you're discouraged or doubting yourself, just remember that God can help you the same way He helped the men and women of the Bible. He is the same yesterday, today, and forever! (See Hebrews 13:8.)

Now these things happened to them as an example and warning [to us]; they were written for our instruction [to admonish and equip us], upon whom the ends of the ages have come.   1 CORINTHIANS 10:11 (AMP)

Sanctification

The act of consecrating or of setting apart for a sacred purpose; consecration

The process of sanctification is one that never completely reaches an end until God calls us from this world and we are completely changed to be just like Him. Until then, we keep growing, and that is all God requires of us.

God wants us to desire His will and work with His Holy Spirit, making progress each day, to accomplish it. As *Vine's Complete Expositionary Dictionary of Old and New Testament Words* says, sanctification is a holiness that is built up little by little through obedience to God's Word.

God is not disappointed because we have not arrived at our desired destination of complete holy character. He is pleased to find us daily pressing on toward the mark of perfection. I find joy in saying, "I'm growing. I am not where I need to be, but thank God I am not where I used to be—I'm okay and I'm on my way."

Now may the God of peace Himself sanctify you completely; and may your whole spirit, soul, and body be preserved blameless at the coming of our Lord Jesus Christ.

1 THESSALONIANS 5:23 (NKJV)

Grateful

Having a due sense of benefits; kindly disposed toward one from whom a favor has been received

---

How thankful you are in the valleys of life helps determine if you'll make it to the mountaintops. When you are tempted to murmur and complain instead of being grateful, keep these things in mind:

- We can complain about what we cannot do, or we can do what we can do.
- We can complain about the conditions in society, or we can pray.

- We can be upset about what we don't have, or we can be grateful for what we do have.
- We can find fault with our friends and family, or we can thank God we are not completely alone.

Gratitude is a matter of proper perspective. I encourage you to take time today to stop and thank God for His blessings and goodness in your life.

O give thanks to the Lord, for He is good; for His mercy and loving-kindness endure forever. PSALM 118:1

Merciful

Compassionate; tender; disposed to pity offenders and to forgive their offenses

---

God is slow to anger and plenteous in mercy (see Psalm 103:8). He is ever ready to forgive us for our sins, and to show us His goodness even when we don't deserve it.

Mercy overrides the rules. You may have grown up in a home that had lots of rules and if you broke any of them, you got into trouble. Although God does intend for us to keep His commands, He understands our nature and is also ready to extend mercy to anyone who will ask for and receive it.

While we may not experience a lot of mercy from people in the world, God does extend it to us at all times.

When we learn to receive mercy, then we will also be able to give it to others. Being merciful is one of the ways we can let Jesus shine through us.

So be merciful (sympathetic, tender, responsive, and compassionate) even as your Father is [all these].   LUKE 6:36

Resolute

Having a fixed purpose; determined; hence, bold; firm; steady; constant in pursuing a purpose

---

The term "analysis paralysis" refers to over-analyzing or overthinking a situation. This complicates the decision-making process. When we seek the one decision that will assure us that perfection will be reached, we can rarely make any decision at all.

I often say that we can think a thing to death. What I mean is that we can suck all the enjoyment out of a thing by overanalyzing it. What could have been a joy turns into an irritation because we are playing mental hockey with it, knocking it all over the place and never making a goal.

If you tend to be indecisive and excessively analytical, resolve to declare war on indecision and bravely go forward with a brand-new decisive attitude. Ask the Lord for wisdom—then make a decision.

> *But Daniel resolved not to defile himself*
> *with the royal food and wine, and he asked*
> *the chief official for permission not to defile*
> *himself this way.*   DANIEL 1:8 (NIV)

Daring

Having courage sufficient for a purpose; challenging; defying

It's not always easy to have a bold dream for what God can do in your life, but it's always worth it. Let me encourage you to take the chance. Don't live a boring, unenthusiastic, little life. Like the apostle Peter, get out of the boat and try to walk on the water (see Matthew 14:22–33).

Don't be afraid of change. Be adventurous and do something you've never done before. Make a decision right now to do the things God has put in your heart, so that at the end of your life you won't look back and have only regret, wishing you had done them but knowing it is too late.

Believe me, being in God's will, and passionately fulfilling His purpose for your life is worth every risk, every uncertainty, and every chance you have to take. Step out in faith and live a daring life today.

Behold, God, my salvation! I will trust and not be afraid, for the Lord God is my strength and song; yes, He has become my salvation.

ISAIAH 12:2

Conversation

Familiar discourse; general intercourse of sentiments; chat; unrestrained talk; opposed to a formal conference

---

Prayer is meant to be a conversation. When you're praying, make sure to listen to what God tells you either through His Word or as a direct revelation to your heart (which will always line up with the Word of God).

Communication is a two-way street. It doesn't consist of one person doing all the talking while the other does all the listening. You may have to develop an ability to listen, but God has some very awesome things to say if we learn to hear Him.

God has invited us into a relationship of fellowship with Him. It is to be an intimate relationship in which we share absolutely everything. God is not someone we visit for one hour on Sunday morning and ignore the rest of the week unless we have an emergency. He is someone we live with. He is our home, and we can be comfortable with Him.

The sheep that are My own hear My voice and listen to Me; I know them, and they follow Me.   JOHN 10:27 (AMP)

Immanuel

**Name of the Messiah as prophesied
by Isaiah, often represented in
Christian exegesis as being Jesus
Christ**

In the Old Testament, the people lived according to the Law. Their only connection to God was through the priest and by trying to keep a series of rules and rituals. They always fell short of what was required so they felt distanced from God. But Jesus came as Immanuel (God with us).

Jesus offered a new way to relate to God: direct, intimate, and personal. And with a new way to relate to God came a new way to live for Him: all mistakes, all sins, and wrongdoing could be forgiven, and each day could bring a new beginning.

Today can be different for you. Today can be a place to begin again! If your life has become full of worry, fear, negative thinking, despair, and regret, today can be a new start. Jesus has forgiven you your sins and offers you new mercies every morning. Receive them and walk with God today!

> *The young woman who is unmarried and a virgin shall conceive and bear a son, and shall call his name Immanuel [God with us].*
>
> ISAIAH 7:14

Enough

A sufficiency; a quantity of a thing that satisfies desire, or is adequate to the want

---

It's so wonderful to have a personal relationship with God because of what Jesus has done for us. The truth is we can never do enough for God no matter how much we do. I know that sounds frustrating and defeating, but it is good news when we realize that Jesus has done all that needs to be done and nothing we can ever do will improve the job He did for us. Jesus was, and is, enough.

True rest comes when we can say, "I don't have to do anything to get God to love and accept me." No matter how good we are, we are never good enough to meet God's standard without Jesus.

As believers, we can present to God all that Jesus is and realize that we stand before God in Christ, and not in ourselves. We have access to the throne of God's grace because of the blood of Christ, and not because of anything we can ever do.

> *. . . In Whom, because of our faith in Him, we dare to have the boldness (courage and confidence) of free access (an unreserved approach to God with freedom and without fear).*   EPHESIANS 3:12

Maximum

The greatest number or quantity attainable in any given case; opposed to minimum

---

John 10:10 shows us that Jesus died for us so we can have abundant life, not a barely-get-by, just-trying-to-get-through-the-day kind of life. Whatever your circumstances are today, the life you have is the only one you have right now, so you might as well learn to love it.

To love the life God has given you means you maximize your potential and step into your destiny.

When you feel good about your life and yourself, it is easier to feel good about the people and things around you. If you have a good attitude in your present situation, God will help you get to where you want to be.

If you really cannot stand your life, then do something about it. Don't just sit and complain—do something to make it better. What do you want out of life? Are you doing something to make it happen, or are you just wishing things were different?

Ask God today for ways to maximize the life He has given you and then step out in boldness to make the most of the day ahead.

I came that they may have and enjoy life, and have it in abundance (to the full, till it overflows).   JOHN 10:10

Power

Force; strength; energy

When Jesus ascended to sit at His Father's right hand until His enemies are made a footstool for His feet (see Luke 20:42–43), He knew we would need power to live the life He had died to provide for us. So He sent us that power in the Holy Spirit.

Just as we learned to lean on Jesus for salvation, we must now learn to lean on the Holy Spirit, Who is the Spirit of grace, for all things that we need in life. As we passionately pursue God's holy character, He provides the strength and ability for change.

Let's say I go to church and hear a

rousing sermon on being kind to my enemies. If I merely go home and try to be
kind, I will fail miserably. But if I go home,
telling God that I am willing but cannot
do it without His help, God will indeed
help me. I have the victory, but God gets
all the credit because I'm victorious as His
power works in me!

*But you shall receive power (ability,
efficiency, and might) when the Holy Spirit
has come upon you, and you shall be My
witnesses in Jerusalem and all Judea and
Samaria and to the ends (the very bounds) of
the earth.*   ACTS 1:8

Exchange

To lay aside, quit, or resign one thing, state, or condition, and take another in the place of it

---

When we enter a relationship with God through Jesus Christ, we are offered an exchanged life. We give Him everything we are and everything we are not, and He gives us everything He is. We give Him our sin, and He gives us His righteousness; we give Him our fears and insecurities, and He gives us His faith and security.

Being a Christian is much more than having our sins forgiven and trying to be good so we can go to heaven when we die. It is a glorious life of freedom, love, faith, righteousness, hope, joy, and peace. It is a life of accomplishment and bearing good fruit through Jesus that glorifies Him. When our security and our identity are in Christ, we do what we do through Him and for Him alone.

You were washed clean (purified by a complete atonement for sin and made free from the guilt of sin), and you were consecrated (set apart, hallowed), and you were justified [pronounced righteous, by trusting] in the name of the Lord Jesus Christ.   1 CORINTHIANS 6:11

Step

To go; to walk a little distance

_____

God has a good plan for our lives, but sometimes obstacles get in the way that keep us from taking the steps He's leading us to take. If there is an area of your life where you are facing fear or anxiety, decide to give it to God and receive His grace to enable you to have faith in that area so you can keep moving forward.

Read, study, and meditate on God's Word about being free from fear and secure in Him. His Word will renew your mind, and fear will turn to faith and courage. Take the steps of faith that God leads you to take even though you might still feel some fear, and as you go forward you will begin to sense more and more freedom.

For example, if you would love to apply for a position that would be a promotion in your company, but you've felt too fearful to do so, step out and try it. Even if you don't get the position, you will have been successful in stepping out in faith, and that is the most important thing. Remember that God is always with you, and as you follow His lead, He delights in your way and busies Himself with your every step!

The steps of a [good] man are directed and established by the Lord when He delights in his way [and He busies Himself with his every step].   PSALM 37:23

Perspective

View; vista

We all have circumstances in our lives that can derail us and prevent us from reaching our goals if we pay excessive attention to them. Do what the crisis demands, but don't give it undue attention. Keep your conversation full of your goals, not your problems.

Scripture teaches us to look away from everything that will distract us and to focus on Jesus who is the Author and the Finisher of our faith (see Hebrews 12:2). This will give us the proper perspective and insight.

It is God who plants goals, dreams, and

visions in our heart, and we can follow His guidance in order to see them brought to completion. Our enemy, the devil, seeks to prevent our progress by providing trials and problems that will distract us if we let them. The solution is simple: do what the crisis demands and choose not to worry about the rest. Cast your care on God and trust Him to see you through.

Looking unto Jesus, the author and finisher of our faith…   HEBREWS 12:2 (NKJV)

Character

The peculiar qualities, impressed by nature or habit on a person . . . these constitute real character, and the qualities he is supposed to possess constitute his estimated character or reputation

---

You may not have realized this, but God thinks you are awesome and that you have great possibilities. He is not blind to your faults, but He looks at them in light of your entire life and not just one event in which you didn't behave well. This is what God says about you:

- You have the mind of Christ,

the ability to think as He thinks
(1 Corinthians 2:16).

- God has accepted you, and He will
  never reject you (Ephesians 2:6).
- You are completely forgiven and
  God has forgotten your sins
  (Hebrews 10:17).
- God created you, and everything
  He created is good (Genesis 1:31).
- God calls you His friend (John
  15:15).
- You are called God's beloved
  (Romans 9:25).

In Christ, there is more right with you
than there is wrong. All you have to do is
look in God's Word to see it.

*The Spirit Himself [thus] testifies together
with our own spirit . . . that we are children
of God.*   ROMANS 8:16

Receiving

Taking; accepting; admitting; embracing; believing; entertaining

---

We conducted a survey at our office, asking our employees what one of their greatest concerns was in their walk with God. The number one response was, "When can I know that I am doing enough?"

Perfectionism is fueled with the tyranny of the *shoulds* and *oughts*. It is the constant nagging feeling of never doing well enough or being good enough. Perfectionists usually have low self-esteem, and they hope that more perfection in their performance will allow them to feel better about themselves. If we never feel quite good enough about ourselves, it is easy to believe that God is not satisfied with us either.

Learning to love yourself is the essence of receiving God's love. It is the ointment that brings healing to your wounded soul. When you receive God's love and learn to love yourself because of it, you'll find rest and be free from the disappointment of perfectionism.

There is no fear in love; but perfect love casts out fear.   1 JOHN 4:18 (NKJV)

Leading

Guiding; conducting; preceding

_____

In order to reach our goals, you and I must follow God's leading.

People will offer us a lot of advice, and some of it may be good, but some of it may not. Or it may be good advice, but simply not what will work for us. It's important that we always look to God first and listen for His guidance and instruction.

God has created us as unique individuals, and He does not lead us all in the same way. So, if you want to win your race, you will need to find your own running style or your own way of doing things.

Of course, we can learn from other

people, but we dare not try to copy them at the cost of losing our own individuality. Appreciate the advice and example of others, but follow God's leading in your life.

The Lord is my Shepherd [to feed, guide, and shield me], I shall not lack... He leads me beside the still and restful waters.

PSALM 23: 1–2

Best

Most good; having good qualities in the highest degree

You were created to have a deep, intimate, personal relationship with God through Jesus Christ and the very best life He came to offer.

Acts 10:34 says, "God shows no partiality and is no respecter of persons." This means His promises apply equally to everyone who follows Him. Yes, you can have the very best God offers, but you can't give up when times get tough. If you'll trust God and follow Him wholeheartedly, you will discover your best life in Him.

God has a great purpose for you, and I urge you not to settle for anything less. He wants to bless you and give you a life that will not only thrill you, fulfill you, and bring you deep joy and sweet satisfaction but also challenge you, stretch you and help you discover that, in Christ, you're stronger than you think.

Every good gift and every perfect (free, large, full) gift is from above; it comes down from the Father.   JAMES 1:17

Guidance

Direction; government; a leading

We all need guidance, especially in the face of a new situation. The first question to ask in a new circumstance is, "Is this God's will for me?" The second question is, "Do I have inner peace about this?"

If we believe we are following God's will, we can trust God to provide everything we need each step of the way.

We follow God by taking one step of obedience after another. As we take each step and see God working, we know it is safe to take another step. It is not wise to merely follow our personal desires, fears, emotions, good ideas, or the advice of others. Acknowledge God in all your ways and He will direct your steps (see Proverbs 3:5–7).

> *And your ears will hear a word behind you, saying, This is the way; walk in it, when you turn to the right hand and when you turn to the left.* ISAIAH 30:21

Motive

That which incites to action; that which determines the choice, or moves the will

---

There are things that God wants us to do. He has called us to bear good fruit, and the apostle John tells us that God is glorified when we bear much, abundant fruit (see John 15:8). But our motive for doing the work is what God is truly interested in.

I want to encourage you to stop and ask yourself why you are doing the various things you do. I love doing what I call "motive checks." It is good to take the time occasionally to ask God to show you anything that you might be doing for a wrong reason.

Don't do things just to please people, but do them because you love God, you trust Him, and you want to obey Him and be a blessing to others.

We speak not to please men but to please God, Who tests our hearts [expecting them to be approved].   1 THESSALONIANS 2:4

Pure

**Genuine; real; true; incorrupt;
unadulterated**

God's eyes roam around the earth searching for someone whose heart is pure before
Him (see 2 Chronicles 16:9). A pure heart
is much more important to the Lord than
a perfect record of good works is.

Although it isn't possible to have perfection in all of our behavior, it is totally possible to have a perfect heart toward God.
A person with a perfect heart is someone
who deeply desires to please God in all
things and is always open to growth and
change that is motivated and led by the
Holy Spirit.

Don't live in fear that you have not done enough and that God is angry with you, or that the door to His presence is closed to you. Ask God to help you develop a pure heart as you trust and believe that the work Jesus did on your behalf was enough.

Create in me a clean heart, O God, and
renew a right, persevering, and steadfast spirit
within me.   PSALM 51:10

Choose

To pick out; to select; to take by way of preference from two or more things offered

---

The first step in doing anything is choosing to do it. In order to forgive, you first choose to forgive. In order to be at peace, you first choose not to worry. In order to start something new, you first choose to step out and go for it.

You may not know how everything is going to work out, but you can make some foundational choices today. Start by saying:

- "Today I choose peace over worry!"

- "Today I choose to break that old habit!"
- "Today I choose not to lash out in anger!"
- "Today I choose not to live in the past!"
- "Today I choose to serve God!"

Make a choice, take a step, and never forget to ask for God's help (His grace) in executing your choice. We can do all things with and through Him, but we can do nothing without Him (see John 15:5; Philippians 4:13).

Choose for yourselves this day whom you will serve. JOSHUA 24:15

Small

Little in amount

The Bible talks a lot about small beginnings. God is a big God—and He can certainly do things quickly when He wants to—but usually He will develop things in our lives through small steps.

God starts small and works up to larger things. He does so in order to help us learn to handle increasing responsibilities and opportunities.

Some of the deepest, richest things God does in your life begin on a small scale—my teaching ministry began with a small home Bible study and now it can potentially reach two-thirds of the world. What we begin with might not impress a crowd, and confetti might not fall from the sky when it happens, but that little thing God is saying to your heart is of utmost importance. I urge you to respect it and do it with excellence.

> *Do not despise these small beginnings, for the Lord rejoices to see the work begin.*
>
> ZECHARIAH 4:10 (NLT)

Trusting

**Confiding in; giving credit;
relying on**

We can trust God for all things. If you need to confront a situation and you're afraid you won't know what to say, then you can ask God to give you the right words at the right time and trust that He will. If you are applying for a job but you're afraid you won't get it, you can ask God for favor and trust that you will get it if it is right for you.

I pray for favor all the time. God's favor causes situations to turn out favorably for you when there is no reason for them to, except that God is working on your behalf.

If you are lonely, ask God to provide friends for you. The situations in which we need God's help are endless, and life can get very exciting when we let Him into all of them through trusting Him, and expecting to see Him work in them.

Blessed (happy, fortunate, to be envied) is the man who makes the Lord his refuge and trust, and turns not to the proud or to followers of false gods.   PSALM 40:4

Abundance

Great plenty; an overflowing quantity

_____

From its opening in Genesis, the Bible tells us a story of abundance. In the first chapter, we see God as lavishly creative. He didn't just create a few stars, He created so many they cannot be counted. His oceans are so huge that we cannot see the end of them from the shore. He created a large variety of animals, plants, flowers, and trees.

And after He made all creation—including man and woman—He said that it was very good. Throughout the Bible we see a God of abundance, who calls Himself *El*

Shaddai, meaning the God of more than enough.

You might say, "I thought we were supposed to be content with what we have." You are right, we are to be content and that means satisfied to the point where we are not disturbed no matter what our circumstances are. But that does not mean we should not trust God to improve our situation and provide for us abundantly.

You crown the year with Your goodness, and
Your paths drip with abundance.

PSALM 65:11 (NKJV)

Planning

Devising a strategy

Man's ways and God's ways are very different from one another. God's ways are better by far, but it often takes us a long time to realize that. And then after that, we have to be willing to give up our old ways of doing things in order to do things God's way.

Proverbs 16:3 says to "roll your works upon the Lord [commit and trust them wholly to Him.]"

Our minds stay very busy planning, and those plans are for what we think will benefit us. But God wants us to roll our works (planning and doing) on Him and follow His plan instead of pushing ahead with ours.

When we acknowledge God in all our ways—including our planning—things work out much better and we have less stress and plenty of joy. It takes some time for us to learn God's ways and be willing to submit to them, but when we do, it is well worth it.

For I know the thoughts and plans that I have for you, says the Lord, thoughts and plans for welfare and peace and not for evil, to give you hope in your final outcome.

JEREMIAH 29:11

Simplicity

**The state of being not complex or
of consisting of few parts**

It is important to develop confidence in simple, believing prayer. We need the confidence that even if we just say, "God, help me," He hears and will answer. We can depend on God to be faithful to do what we have asked Him to do, as long as our request is in accordance with His will. The Holy Spirit is called our Helper, and He delights in helping us.

Too often we get caught up in our own works concerning prayer. Sometimes we try to pray so long, loud, and eloquently that we lose sight of the fact that prayer is simply conversation with God. The length or loudness or eloquence of our prayer is not the issue; what is important is the sincerity of our heart and the confidence we have that God hears and will answer us.

And when you pray, do not heap up phrases (multiply words, repeating the same ones over and over) as the Gentiles do, for they think they will be heard for their much speaking.

MATTHEW 6:7

Stand

To remain upright, in a moral sense; not to fall

There are going to be plenty of times when people or circumstances will try to hold you back from God's best in your life. But God is with you, in you, and He is your strength.

God will help you stand firm and be determined to go forward no matter who or what is coming against you. It may not always be easy, but being frustrated and unfulfilled due to being outside the will of God is more difficult than pressing through all the opposition in order to walk in His will.

Through Christ you can have a quiet, inner confidence that takes you through to the finish line. Confidence in God is knowing that despite adverse circumstances, everything will work out for your good in the end. You have had victories in the past and you will have many more in the future.

Therefore take up the whole armor of God, that you may be able to withstand in the evil day, and having done all, to stand. Stand therefore.   EPHESIANS 6:13–14 (NKJV)

Adventure

**An enterprise of hazard; a bold
undertaking, in which hazards are
to be encountered, and the issue is
staked upon unforeseen events**

God loves you and He has a wonderful
plan for your life. Whatever it is He is calling you to do, God will make you able to
do it. You do not have to *feel* able, and you
do not have to have experience in that area.
All you need is a right motive and a heart
full of faith. God is not looking for ability;
He is looking for availability. He is looking for somebody to say, "Here I am, God,
send me. I want to serve You, God. I want
to do something for You!"

The truth is, we weren't created to do the same things all of our lives. God has put a craving for adventure in us, and adventure means trying something we have never done before. Adventure means stepping out in faith, doing something different, and not always living in your comfort zone. If you want God to use you, don't let a fear of the unknown hold you back.

Also I heard the voice of the Lord, saying,
Whom shall I send? And who will go for Us?
Then said I, Here am I; send me.

ISAIAH 6:8

Persevere

To persist in any business or enterprise undertaken

With God on your side, the only way you can lose is if you quit. So no matter what happens, no matter what it looks like in the natural, no matter what lie the enemy tries to tell you, *refuse to give up*!

Sometimes the most spiritual thing you can say is, "I'm not going to give up! I'm going to be obedient, walk in faith, and wait for God's victory."

- When people say bad things about you, *refuse to give up.*

- When something looks impossible, *refuse to give up*.
- When things appear to get worse instead of better, *refuse to give up*.

Perseverance will bring you through to a place of victory. When you persevere, you'll find that God has been in control the entire time. He may have taken you on a different route than you would have chosen, but He will use even that for your good and for your spiritual growth.

If we endure, we shall also reign with Him.

2 TIMOTHY 2:12

Attitude

Mental disposition; view toward a situation or person

If there is no noticeable difference between the attitude of a believer and the attitude of a nonbeliever, something is wrong. We believers are called to be the light of the world; something has to be different about us, and I believe that one of the ways we show that difference is with our attitudes.

The kind of attitude we have toward everything in life is extremely important. Your attitude belongs to you and no one can make you have a bad one if you don't want to. Also, no one can make you have a good one unless you choose to do so.

In every situation, choose to have the same attitude you believe Jesus would, and you can enjoy your life even in difficult and challenging times.

Do all things without complaining and disputing, that you may become blameless and harmless, children of God without fault in the midst of a crooked and perverse generation, among whom you shine as lights in the world. PHILIPPIANS 2:14–15 (NKJV)

Example

A pattern; a copy; a model; that which is proposed to be imitated

---

People believe a lot more of what they see you do than what they hear you say. That's why it is important that we take the responsibility to set a good, biblical example. How we live in front of people and even behind closed doors at home is essential to being an effective witness.

Don't just tell others what to do; let them see you set the example. If a parent tells a child to have good manners and then the child sees Mom and Dad being rude to one another, they have wasted their words.

The Bible says we should "watch and pray" (see Mark 14:38). I think we need to watch ourselves a little more and pray we will live out the faith we so boldly profess. When we set the right example, it is an effective illustration of our faith.

Let no one despise or think less of you because of your youth, but be an example (pattern) for the believers in speech, in conduct, in love, in faith, and in purity. 1 TIMOTHY 4:12

Invest

To confer; to give

To really enjoy your life, it is important for you to avoid becoming stagnant and inactive. If you've ever seen a puddle of stagnant water, you know it's murky and smelly, and there may even be some mold forming on it. Well, the same thing can happen in your life.

No matter how enthusiastic you once were, you can become stagnant if you don't invest and do your part to keep yourself stirred up.

Stagnation can occur in marriage, on the job, at church, at school, in your personal life, in your spiritual life, and in many other areas. Stagnation happens when we stop investing in these areas. In order to keep every area of your life fresh and living, take the time to stir them up. Plan a surprise for your spouse, be thankful for your job, find a new ministry to serve in at church—whatever the Lord leads you to do, invest your time and energy and He will always keep things fresh and adventurous.

I would remind you to stir up (rekindle the embers of, fan the flame of, and keep burning) the [gracious] gift of God.   2 TIMOTHY 1:6

Accept

To receive with favor; to approve

Many people will want to attach themselves to you when you are moving up in life—when you are doing something others think is good or when you are gaining visibility, prestige, or respect. But when you do something unpopular or out of the ordinary, you may lose some friends.

If you want to do anything great for God, you may have to be willing to endure rejection and loneliness for a while. It is worthwhile, though, and in the end, you will be glad you pressed through.

Realize that no matter how much rejection you face, God accepts you completely.

He wants you to break through the bar-
rier of rejection and keep making progress
toward your goals.

*All whom My Father gives (entrusts) to Me
will come to Me; and the one who comes to
Me I will most certainly not cast out [I will
never, no never, reject one of them who comes
to Me].*   JOHN 6:37

Sacrifice

Surrender of anything for the sake of something else

When God asks us to do something, we often ask: *What is this going to cost me? What do I have to give up? If I do this, how uncomfortable am I going to be?*

The truth is that anything that is really worth doing requires a sacrifice, especially anything we do for God. Part of loving and serving Him involves a willingness to lay down our lives for Him.

Do not be afraid of sacrifice when God calls you or puts a dream in your heart. Whatever it is you have to lay down or give up is nothing compared to the reward that comes with obeying His guidance. God's plan for you is greater than anything you can imagine. Every sacrifice you make as you follow His guidance will bring increased peace and joy in your life.

Make a decisive dedication of your bodies [presenting all your members and faculties] as a living sacrifice, holy (devoted, consecrated) and well pleasing to God, which is your reasonable (rational, intelligent) service and spiritual worship.   ROMANS 12:1

Stronger

Well fortified; able to sustain attacks; not easily subdued or taken

---

We all face obstacles from time to time. God doesn't remove every obstacle that stands in our way because we are often made stronger as we learn to overcome obstacles.

When we deal with the difficulties of life, we are strengthened. But if we run from all of them, we will never grow and become stronger in our faith and abilities.

If God allowed us to go through all of life without any obstacles, it would harm us. We would not be as strong as we could have been. Many times our obstacles are what God uses to give us the strength to succeed, as long as we refuse to quit when there seems to be no way to go on.

You can face your fears and overcome them, and when you do, you'll often find they gave you the strength you needed for the next situation that comes.

Let us exult and triumph in our troubles
and rejoice in our sufferings, knowing that
pressure and affliction and hardship produce
patient and unswerving endurance.

ROMANS 5:3

Assurance

Firmness of mind; undoubting steadiness

"Trust me." Have you ever heard those two words and when you heard them, you really wanted to trust but something inside said, *Be careful*...or even *Beware*?

Broken trust is perhaps one of the strongest sources of hurt, disappointment, and pain we can experience. But the good news is that we have this assurance: God can be trusted. He will never hurt you.

When it seems everyone else has abandoned us, we have the assurance that God is with us (see Matthew 28:20). When things aren't going our way, we have the assurance God will cause all things to work together for our good (see Romans 8:28).

No matter how difficult things look around you, rest in the assurance that God is trustworthy, and He will see you through.

Then shall they know [positively] that I, the Lord their God, am with them. EZEKIEL 34:30

Conquer

To overcome, as difficulties; to surmount, as obstacles; to subdue whatever opposes

---

God's Word says that we are more than conquerors. To me, that means we choose to believe we can, with God's help, overcome anything that stands in our way. It is amazingly freeing and good to know that we can overcome problems *before* we even have them.

Are you dreading things that have not even taken place yet? If you are, you don't have to because you can adopt the attitude of a conqueror. You can replace those dreads with a confident attitude that says,

"No matter what comes my way in life, I can face it and overcome it with God's help."

This kind of confidence opens the door to a life that you can thoroughly enjoy.

We are more than conquerors and gain
a surpassing victory through Him Who
loved us.   ROMANS 8:37

Connected

Being joined in close association

If you want to live a peaceful, joy-filled, abundant life, you need to understand it all begins with the thoughts you choose to think. Your mind is connected to every feeling you have and every action you take.

A worried, anxious life begins with thoughts like this: *How am I going to do everything I have to do? My life is impossible! This is more than I can handle!*

But a contented, happy life begins with thoughts like this: *God loves me, and He will take care of everything in my future. He will give me the strength and ability to do each thing I need to do as it comes up.*

You can choose the thoughts you want to dwell on. Your mind is connected to every part of your life, so choose to focus on godly thoughts today in order to experience the life Jesus came to give you.

You will guard him and keep him in perfect
and constant peace whose mind [both its
inclination and its character] is stayed
on You.   ISAIAH 26:3

Mature

Completed; prepared; ready

I often say that there are two types of faith, and I believe we need both of them. One is the type of faith that asks for and receives an immediate pleasurable answer. God delivers quickly and miraculously, and we get very excited. The second type of faith is one that doesn't receive the answer it had hoped for, but continues to believe anyway that God is good and that He is working in ways that cannot yet be seen.

Although not as emotionally exciting, the second type of faith, in my personal opinion, is the greater faith—the more mature faith.

We don't get to choose which way God will work. At times He delivers us from something difficult, and at other times He gives us the grace to endure it with a good attitude. What God does or does not allow us to go through is His decision alone, but it is always a decision that will lead to God's very best in our lives.

The fountain of skillful and godly Wisdom is like a gushing stream [sparkling, fresh, pure, and life-giving].   PROVERBS 18:4

Patient

Persevering; constant in pursuit or exertion; calmly diligent

---

The best way to damage a relationship is to look at the other person and think, *You will never change.* Thankfully, God always believes we can change, and therefore, He continues to work with us.

We would be more patient and long-suffering with the flaws of people if we purposely thought, *God is patient with me and I will be patient with you.* We can always choose to pray for people instead of giving up on them.

Nobody is beyond change. It may take a long time for them to do so, but with

God's help it can happen. Even if you see no change at all yet, continue believing that God is working, and guide your conversations with others in that direction. Fill your mind with thoughts like *I believe God is working and all things are possible with Him*. You will feel better, and your attitude toward others will be much better.

> *With patience, bearing with one another*
> *and making allowances because you love one*
> *another...*   EPHESIANS 4:2

Help

**To aid; to assist; to lend strength or
means toward effecting a purpose**

The early church, which we read about
in the book of Acts, was a very powerful church. It shook the known world of
its time, and its influence is still being felt
around the world today. It was unified,
and all the people who were part of it were
busy helping the people they knew who
were in need. The people in the church
helped those they knew personally and
those they heard about in other towns and
cities through the apostles who came to
visit and teach them.

The early church grew rapidly and had

a wonderful reputation because it was filled with people who genuinely loved one another. What the world needs is love, not religion. It needs God, and God is love. If we simply decide to love and help those in need, we'll be amazed at how we can change our world.

But do not forget to do good and to share, for with such sacrifices God is well pleased.

HEBREWS 13:16 (NKJV)

Boldness

Confidence; confident trust

If we are going to do anything great for God and be determined to pursue the dreams He places in our hearts, we have to be bold enough to take chances; we have to be courageous. Life isn't always easy, but we don't have to stop or quit when we face a problem. With God's help, we can confidently press ahead.

When we face situations that threaten or intimidate, it's important that we pray for God to give us a courageous spirit and an inner boldness to overcome the obstacle.

Fear will always try to keep us from

going forward. But we can overcome fear with God's help. It is a misconception to think that courageous people don't feel fear; they press on even though the feeling of fear is still present. Boldness says, *God is on my side, and if He is for me, it doesn't matter who or what stands against me!*

We have confidence (complete assurance and boldness) before God.   1 JOHN 3:21

Forgive

To pardon; to remit; as an offense or debt; to overlook an offense, and treat the offender as not guilty

---

As long as we live, we will encounter people who offend us, disappoint us, hurt us, reject us, use the wrong tone of voice with us, or let us down in times of need. Those dynamics are just part of human nature, and they come with the territory of relationships.

But as Christians we can learn to forgive people when they hurt us rather than hold on to anger and resentment. When we forgive, we are actually doing ourselves a favor. We are freeing ourselves from the agony of bitter thoughts.

Why should we ruin our lives over other people's bad behavior? Instead, we can take the high road and forgive—just as God has forgiven us.

Then Peter came up to Him and said, Lord, how many times may my brother sin against me and I forgive him and let it go? [As many as] up to seven times? Jesus answered him, I tell you, not up to seven times, but seventy times seven!   MATTHEW 18:21–22

Unstuck

Free

_____

I've noticed there are a lot of Christians stuck on the starting blocks of life. They aren't sure how a situation is going to turn out, or exactly what they should do, so they do nothing. Instead of running the race God has set before them (see Hebrews 12:1), they are letting worry and anxiety keep them frozen at the starting line.

God wants you to participate in the miracle He is doing in your life. If you think you're going to wake up one day and supernaturally be at the finish line, you're going to be disappointed. It doesn't work that way.

Faith is always active—always. It requires that you move forward into what God is telling you to do. Don't neglect to take a step because you're afraid it will be the wrong one. Living in fear all the time and making no decision is much worse than being decisive and occasionally making a mistake.

You shall walk in all the ways which the Lord your God has commanded you, that you may live and that it may go well with you and that you may live long in the land which you shall possess.   DEUTERONOMY 5:33

Anywhere

At or in or to any place

_____

God can show up in your life and speak to you anywhere. I still remember when God called me into the ministry. I was in my room, making my bed. I sensed the Lord say, _Joyce, you are going to go all over the place and share My Word._ It wasn't an audible voice, but it might as well have been; it was that clear.

It's not where you are or what you are doing in the moment that changes you— I was doing the average, ordinary task of making my bed—it's the power of God in that moment that changes you. And that can happen anytime and anywhere.

It is a mistake to think that God can only speak to us if we are doing something we consider to be spiritual. God is with us all the time, in every place. So be expectant today—God can speak to you anywhere!

Where could I go from Your Spirit? Or where could I flee from Your presence? If I ascend up into heaven, You are there; if I make my bed in Sheol (the place of the dead), behold, You are there.   PSALM 139:7–8

Persistence

**Steady pursuit of what is
undertaken**

God will make a way for us to do everything He places in our hearts. He does not
put dreams and visions in us to frustrate us.
We can keep our confidence and persist all
the way through to the end, no matter how
big the mountain in front of us appears.

God does not usually call people who
are capable on their own; if He did, He
would not get the glory. He frequently
chooses those who feel they are completely
in over their heads but who are ready to
take bold steps of faith as they get direction from God.

We usually want to wait until we feel ready before we step out, but if we feel ready then we tend to lean on ourselves instead of on God. Know your weaknesses and know God—know His strength and faithfulness. Above all else, don't quit. Be persistent and you'll see God do something amazing in your life.

And as for you, brethren, do not become weary or lose heart in doing right [but continue in well-doing without weakening].

2 THESSALONIANS 3:13

Habit

A disposition or condition of the mind or body acquired by custom or a frequent repetition of the same act

---

We all have habits. Some of them are good and some are bad. The good ones benefit us and add joy and power to our lives, while the bad ones do nothing but steal our peace and joy and prevent our success.

Good habits can be developed, and any bad habit can be broken, through repetition. The experts say that a habit can be formed or broken in thirty days, so I encourage you to give it a try and decide to change your life by changing any bad habits.

At first it may be difficult, but as you find your strength in Christ to keep going (see Philippians 4:13), diligence and patience will eventually bring success. Good habits can be developed and benefit your life if you are consistent and determined to make daily progress. So let go of those habits that are harmful or distracting and start developing habits that will help you succeed.

But his delight and desire are in the law of the Lord, and on His law (the precepts, the instructions, the teachings of God) he habitually meditates (ponders and studies) by day and by night.   PSALM 1:2

Transformed

Changed in form or external appearance; metamorphosed; transmuted; renewed

---

New birth in Christ happens the instant we ask Jesus to forgive our sins and be our Savior, but *learning to live a new life* is a process of transformation.

God doesn't work just with our behavior; He also changes our hearts. When we seriously commit ourselves to Jesus as Savior and Lord, God begins transforming us from the inside out. He makes us like Jesus on the inside and wants to work what is in us so it shows on the *outside* and other people can see and experience Jesus through us.

This transformation doesn't happen overnight and will seem very slow at times. When you are tempted to condemn yourself because you aren't making the progress you think you should be making, remind yourself, "I'm okay and I'm on my way!" Remember that through faith you have been made right with God, and even though you have not arrived at perfection, you are making progress.

For both He Who sanctifies [making men holy] and those who are sanctified all have one [Father]. For this reason He is not ashamed to call them brethren.   HEBREWS 2:11

Guiltless

free from guilt; innocent

God will convict us of wrong choices and actions, but He never tries to make us feel guilty. Guilt presses down and weakens us, but godly conviction brings awareness of wrong, and an opportunity to change and progress.

We are not built for guilt. Had God wanted us to feel guilty, He would not have sent Jesus to redeem us from guilt. Jesus paid for our sins and the guilt they cause (see Isaiah 53:6 and 1 Peter 2:24–25).

As believers in Jesus Christ, and as sons and daughters of God, we have been set free from the power of sin (see Romans

6:6–10). That doesn't mean we'll never sin, but it does mean that when we do, we can admit it, receive forgiveness, and be free from guilt and condemnation.

But we believe that we are saved through the grace (the undeserved favor and mercy) of the Lord Jesus, just as they [are].   ACTS 15:11

Overlook

To pass by indulgently; to excuse; not to punish or censure

Some people say over and over, "I am just touchy, and I get my feelings hurt easily. That is just the way I am, and I cannot help it." This is what they believe about themselves, and this belief controls their words and actions, which is so unfortunate because it is just an excuse to continue in this harmful behavior.

I cannot stress enough how important it is to become a person who overlooks offenses. Being offended will prevent us from making spiritual progress. If we are focused on who we are angry with and what they did to offend us, then we cannot focus on God's Word and His plan for us, and we will not grow spiritually.

Be wise enough to realize that being offended is a trap; don't take the bait.

Hatred stirs up contentions, but love covers all transgressions.   PROVERBS 10:12

Guide

To lead or direct in a way; to conduct in a course or path

God will try to guide us, but He won't force us to do the right thing or to move in the direction He has set forth for us.

Anything God guides us to do or not to do is for our benefit, and if we trust that, then we can follow His direction more easily. God's desire is that we want His will more than we want anything else. There is no better place to be than in the will of God.

The center of God's will is a place of joy, peace, and rest. When these things are missing in our lives it may be a strong indication that we have slipped out of God's will. However, God will guide us back to the right path if we ask Him to.

You in Your mercy and loving-kindness have led forth the people whom You have redeemed; You have guided them in Your strength to Your holy habitation.   EXODUS 15:13

Waiting

Staying in expectation

_____

Waiting for God to do what only God can do is one of the most difficult parts of faith. Our timing and His are usually two completely different things.

God promises to never be late and even states that He is not slow as man defines slowness (see 2 Peter 3:9). But usually He isn't early, and we do have to wait. It is important to wait with a good attitude and trust that God's time is the right time.

As you wait on God, expect something good to happen at any moment. That will allow you to enjoy the wait instead of being sour and miserable.

But those who wait for the Lord [who expect, look for, and hope in Him] shall change and renew their strength and power; they shall lift their wings and mount up [close to God] as eagles [mount up to the sun]; they shall run and not be weary, they shall walk and not faint or become tired. ISAIAH 40:31

Refreshing

Relief after fatigue or suffering

We all need times of blessed quiet because we can find physical, emotional, and spiritual refreshing in those times.

We live in a noisy world, and if we are not careful we can become addicted to noise and constant activity. Make sure you find time in your life to just be quiet and listen.

Are you asking God to speak to you, but you never take the time to get quiet and just listen? It honors God when we give Him regular time. Sit with Him and enjoy His Presence—it will be refreshing to your entire being.

Time is one of the most important things we can give God. It tells Him He is important to us and that we realize we cannot manage life properly without Him.

Return [to God], that your sins may be erased (blotted out, wiped clean), that times of refreshing (of recovering from the effects of heat, of reviving with fresh air) may come from the presence of the Lord.   ACTS 3:19

Tenacious

Holding fast, or inclined to hold fast; inclined to retain what is in possession

---

When facing difficulties in life, instead of becoming discouraged, you can use those difficulties and obstacles as stepping-stones to your goals in life.

If a seemingly impossible situation comes your way, do not just allow it to defeat you. Be tenacious about overcoming it, through your faith in Christ, and determined to make it work for you, not against you. Let the circumstances that could suffocate you be the very situations that strengthen you and raise you to a new level.

Be a person who is willing to work with God to develop a determined "can do" attitude; act on the truth that His power is at work within you and that you can do all things you need to do in life through Christ (see Philippians 4:13).

Let us hold fast our confession [of faith in Him].　　　HEBREWS 4:14

Legacy

A bequest; a particular thing or certain sum of money given by last will or testament

---

As a child of God, His Spirit dwells in you, and all that He is is available to you through faith in Him. You can know God and have intimate fellowship with Him. You can live a life that will leave a legacy of faith in Him for others.

God loves you, and He has created you in a unique and special way. No one can do what you can do, exactly the way you can do it. God wants you to learn to make the most of every moment in your life and to have a good influence on the next generation.

If you make good choices in life it will enable you not only to enjoy your own life but to be a great example for those who are younger than you. The apostle Paul was a great example to his spiritual son Timothy, and he enjoyed seeing him serve God and do mighty things.

As you invest in others, your own life will be much richer and more rewarding.

We will tell to the generation to come the praiseworthy deeds of the Lord, and His might, and the wonderful works that He has performed. PSALM 78:4

Accomplish

To complete; to finish entirely

One of the reasons many people do not enjoy life, or miss out on some of the blessings God wants to give them, is that their lives are cluttered with unfinished projects. They never taste the joy of accomplishing a goal or fulfilling a desire because they do not press past the challenges that arise.

Every person has an excuse bag. It's a little invisible accessory we carry around with us, and when something that seems difficult arises, challenging us or giving us more than we want to deal with, we pull out an excuse. *That is just too hard...I*

*don't have enough time...I don't have any-
one to help me...I'm afraid.*

I urge you to throw away your excuse
bag. Go get a "can do" bag and fill it
with biblical, faith-filled reasons you can
accomplish what you want to accomplish
in your life.

> *Thus Solomon finished the Lord's house and
> the king's house; all that [he] had planned to
> do in the Lord's house and his own house he
> accomplished successfully.*
>
> 2 CHRONICLES 7:11

Balance

**To regulate different powers, so
as to keep them in a state of just
proportion**

The Bible says everything is beautiful in
its time (see Ecclesiastes 3:11). Something
may not be bad in itself, but if the timing
of it is off for us, that makes it bad for that
particular season in our lives. At another
time it may be perfectly permissible and
something we should do.

I have found staying balanced in life
and doing enough of a thing but not too
much of it, is one of the greatest challenges
we face. Some people tend to do too much
of everything. They work too much, spend

too much money, or even talk too much. We need to do all of those things, but if they are done in excess, they can become big problems. Seek balance and be open to letting God show you what needs to be changed.

[He has given us a spirit] of power and of love and of calm and well-balanced mind and discipline and self-control.   2 TIMOTHY 1:7

Confrontation

**The act of bringing two persons
into the presence of each other
for examination and discovery
of truth**

People who devalue themselves and have
a root of rejection don't handle confrontation or any kind of correction very well.
They usually become defensive and try
to convince the people confronting them
that they are wrong in their assessment of
them.

No one enjoys being told they are
wrong about something and that they
need to change, but a secure individual
can handle it much better than an insecure

one. Accepting God's love and approval and being rooted in it will help us receive confrontation with a good attitude. The person confronting us may or may not be right, but at least we can listen without becoming angry.

When we truly know our worth and value as a child of God, it won't upset us when someone else mentions a fault they think we have. Ask God to help you handle confrontation graciously.

Iron sharpens iron; so a man sharpens the countenance of his friend [to show rage or worthy purpose].   PROVERBS 27:17

Completely

Fully; perfectly; entirely

When I talk about God's forgiveness, I like to use the term "complete forgiveness" because I want to stress that God's forgiveness is not partial or almost; it is complete.

When someone has sinned against us, we may forgive a little but still hold some kind of grudge. This, of course, is not true forgiveness at all. The God-kind of forgiveness is complete.

Take a moment and think of the worst thing you can remember that you have ever done. Now, realize that you are *completely* forgiven. The goodness of God is greater than any bad thing we have ever done or could ever do. That should bring a sigh of relief and a sensation of joy sweeping through your soul.

For You, O Lord, are good, and ready to forgive [our trespasses, sending them away, letting them go completely and forever]; and You are abundant in mercy and loving-kindness to all those who call upon You.

PSALM 86:5

Newness

Different state or qualities introduced by change or regeneration

---

God goes to great lengths in His Word to inform us that, in Christ, we are new creatures, old things have passed away, and all things have become new (2 Corinthians 5:17).

In Christ, we are offered a brand-new way of living. We have newness of life—a new covenant with God sealed in the blood of Jesus.

Jesus gave us one new commandment: that we should love one another as He loves us (see John 13:34). Everything that

God offers is new. Every old thing can be left behind. Your future has no room in it for your past mistakes. Actually, your future is so bright that you need sunglasses to look at it!

Therefore if any person is [ingrafted] in Christ (the Messiah) he is a new creation (a new creature altogether); the old [previous moral and spiritual condition] has passed away. Behold, the fresh and new has come!

2 CORINTHIANS 5:17

Loving

**Entertaining a strong affection for;
having tender regard for**

All of us make mistakes. All of us have weaknesses. But God doesn't want us to focus on what is wrong with people—He wants us to pray for them and love them!

Being Jesus' disciple means being kind to others, tenderhearted, understanding, loving, and forgiving. I've also realized it often means overlooking their weaknesses and shortcomings. If we truly love others as Christ loves us, this is something we can do by God's grace.

The main thing people are looking for is love. Most of the time they look for that love in all the wrong places, but if they do look to the church or to a Christian, they should not be disillusioned and disappointed. Jesus said they would know us by our love.

By this shall all [men] know that you are My disciples, if you love one another [if you keep on showing love among yourselves].

JOHN 13:35

Sleep

To take rest by a suspension of the voluntary exercise of the powers of the body and mind

Taking care of our bodies is very important, because they are God's home. There are several simple things we can do to ensure better health and increased energy, but the most important thing is to sleep seven or eight hours every night.

Some people mistreat their bodies by never getting enough sleep and eating excessive amounts of foods that are unhealthy or not drinking enough water. Then, if they get really sick, they usually pray and ask God for healing, without ever realizing their poor choices are the root cause of their problem.

God is merciful and He is our healer, but He also expects us to live a balanced lifestyle and use common sense. Our bodies are precious, marvelous gifts from God, and we should respect them and take good care of them.

I lay down and slept; I wakened again, for the Lord sustains me.   PSALM 3:5

Fearless

Bold; intrepid; undaunted

Fear is the opposite of faith. We receive from the enemy through fear, and we receive from God through faith. Fear is the enemy's brand of faith, his counterfeit. In other words, we can know and do God's will through placing our faith in Him, but we can cooperate with the devil's plan through fear.

When we are afraid, we may fail to do what God wants us to do and instead end up doing what the devil wants us to do. In the Old Testament, Job said that what he feared came upon him (see Job 3:25), which is exactly what the enemy wanted for him and what he wants for us.

The enemy is the author of fear, not God. In fact, 2 Timothy 1:7 says God has not given us a spirit of fear but of power, and we need to apply this truth to our lives and refuse to live any way other than boldly and courageously.

Do not, therefore, fling away your fearless confidence, for it carries a great and glorious compensation of reward.   HEBREWS 10:35

Repent

In theology, to sorrow or be pained for sin, as a violation of God's holy law

---

Peace with God is maintained by never attempting to hide sin. We must always come clean with God and keep good communication open between us and Him.

When we make mistakes, we don't ever have to withdraw from God. Rather, we can come near because only He can restore us. To repent means we turn away from sin and return to the highest place.

God is not surprised by our weaknesses and failures. Actually, He knew about the mistakes we would make before we made them. All we need to do is admit them and He is faithful to forgive us continually from all sin (see 1 John 1:9).

Repent (think differently; change your mind, regretting your sins and changing your conduct), for the kingdom of heaven is at hand.   MATTHEW 3:2

Plenty

Abundance; copiousness; full or adequate supply

———————

As a child of God, there is no such thing as not enough.

You may think, "I don't have enough talent; the *only* thing I know how to do is…" or, "I didn't accomplish everything I wanted for the Lord today. The *only* thing I did was…" or maybe even, "I can't think of much to be joyful about today. The *only* thing I can think of is so small that it is *not enough*."

God looks at your "not enough" and says, *No problem! I'm more than enough!*

Those small things that seem insignificant

to you are infinite in the hands of God. He can do a miracle with every little thing you give Him. God can take your "not enough" and turn it into His *plenty*!

> *He took the five loaves and the two fish, and, looking up to heaven, He gave thanks and blessed and broke the loaves and handed the pieces to the disciples, and the disciples gave them to the people.*   MATTHEW 14:19

Restored

Returned; brought back; retrieved; recovered; cured; renewed; reestablished

---

God can restore anything in your life—it's never too late. Mary and Martha thought it was too late for Jesus to help Lazarus because he had been dead for four days and was beginning to decay by the time Jesus showed up. But Lazarus was raised from the dead by the power of God. In your life, no matter what the need is, it's never too late for God to bring restoration:

- You can still have a great marriage.
- You can still get out of debt.

- You can still be the parent you've always wanted to be.
- You can still evict worry and anxiety from your home.
- You can still live a stress-free, happy life.

In everything and in every area of your life, it's never too late with God.

So I will restore to you the years that the swarming locust has eaten.

JOEL 2:25 (NKJV)

Filled

**Made full; supplied with
abundance**

I learned a long time ago that I could try
to fix my problems in my own strength or
I could give them to God—but I couldn't
do both. And when I began to turn over
my struggles and frustrations to God, not
only did He take care of each situation in
His perfect timing, but I felt completely
different. Instead of being filled with anxiety, anger or disappointment, I was filled
with God's peace and His joy!

What about you? What is going on in
your life that you might be trying to fix

in your own strength? Is your heart filled
with worry or is it filled with peace?

If you feel like you're carrying a burden,
Jesus gives you this promise: *Come to Me,
all you who labor and are heavy-laden and
overburdened, and I will cause you to rest*
(Matthew 11:28).

> *When You give it to them, they gather it up;*
> *You open Your hand, and they are filled with*
> *good things.*   PSALM 104:28

Compliment

An expression of praise, admiration, or congratulation

One of the easiest ways to show love is to decide to make others feel valuable.

I have discovered that most people we meet or come into contact with in our everyday lives do not have a sense of their infinite value as children of God. They feel devalued and worthless, but we can change that by building people up, by encouraging and edifying them. One way to do this is with a sincere compliment, which is one of the most valuable gifts in the world.

Making another person feel valuable

isn't expensive and doesn't have to be time consuming. Develop a habit of aggressively looking for things you can say to others that will add value to their life. Offering a sincere compliment may seem like a small thing, but it gives tremendous strength.

Therefore encourage (admonish, exhort) one another and edify (strengthen and build up) one another, just as you are doing.

1 THESSALONIANS 5:11

Why

For what cause or reason

I like to define a motive as "the *why* behind the *what*." A motive is the reason we do what we do. It is easy to say *what* we are doing with our time, but sometimes we do not understand *why* we do what we do. We might be doing something just to be well thought of, when truly we don't have the time to do it.

Impure motives can cause many problems, one of which is being overcommitted, which results in unnecessary stress in our lives. Surely we won't live with extreme stress if we are obeying God and doing only what He wants us to do.

Never agree to do something in order to impress people or because you fear what they may think or say about you if you don't. When an opportunity comes up, take the motive test—ask yourself, "Why am I doing this? Is this something I'm doing for God or something I'm doing to please people?"

> *Every man's way is right in his own eyes, but the Lord weighs and examines the hearts [of people and their motives].*
>
> PROVERBS 21:2 (AMP)

Unexpected

Not looked for; sudden

Learning to expect the unexpected isn't having a negative attitude; it is simply accepting that we cannot control all of life and then trusting that God will enable us to deal with things as they come.

One time, I decided to keep a log of the unexpected things that happened to me over an eight-week period of time. I logged thirty-three things that interrupted my plan and that I had to deal with. I had no choice—they were staring me in the face and I couldn't avoid them. I couldn't control them, but I could control my response to them.

Not only can we learn to expect the unexpected but we can refuse to fear the unexpected. We can live with a confident attitude that God will give us the ability to deal with whatever we need to deal with in life. He has promised to never let more come on us than we can bear and to always provide a way out (see 1 Corinthians 10:13).

You are the God of my salvation; for You [You only and altogether] do I wait [expectantly] all the day long.   PSALM 25:5

Deliberate

**Weighing facts and arguments
with a view to a choice or decision**

I believe we should have a think session every day. If we were to sit down regularly and say to ourselves, "I am going to think about a few things for a few minutes," and then deliberately think about some of the things the Bible tells us to think about, our lives would improve dramatically. Disciplining ourselves to think properly by having on-purpose think sessions will train us to begin thinking better in our everyday lives.

We think about a variety of things every day, but most of us need to deliberately and purposefully change the content of our thoughts. Instead of thinking, *I'm no good; I mess up everything; I never do anything right*, we can use our mental energy to think about how much God loves us and how we are in a right relationship with Him through Jesus Christ. As you spend more time enjoying purposeful think sessions, great transformation will take place in your life.

*And set your minds and keep them set on
what is above (the higher things), not on the
things that are on the earth.*

COLOSSIANS 3:2

Can

**Have means, or instruments,
which supply power or ability**

———————————

No matter how many times you have heard someone say to you, "You can't," I want to say to you, "Oh, yes you can!" I believe that miracles come in "cans"—our belief that we can do whatever we need to do through Christ, Who is our strength.

I believe in you; God believes in you; and it's time for you to believe in yourself. Today is a new day! Put the past and all its negative, discouraging comments behind you. Believe that anything is possible with God.

Negative words and words that speak

of failure come from the enemy, not from God, so decide right now not to allow the power of "you can't" to influence you anymore. Choose to agree with God and say to yourself, "I can!" And let the power of God's positive promises outweigh the power of the negative words anyone has ever spoken over you.

I can do all things through Christ who strengthens me.   PHILIPPIANS 4:13 (NKJV)

Fresh

New; recently grown

Because Jesus lived a perfect life, died for our sins, and was raised from the dead, we no longer live under the old covenant of the Law, works, sin, and death. He has provided a fresh, new life for us. We are instructed to let go of what lies behind in order to make way for the new.

Jesus said that new wine could not be poured into old wineskins. That tells us that the new life that God has for us has no room for the old way of living in it. We must leave behind old ways of thinking and old behavior patterns.

Just doing a Bible study on all the things

that God has made new is very encouraging. Are you holding on to old things while at the same time trying to live a new life in Christ? If so, you will only feel frustrated and defeated. Instead of living that way, choose to embrace your new life in Christ. Remember that in Him, every day can be a new beginning.

And be constantly renewed in the spirit of your mind [having a fresh mental and spiritual attitude].   EPHESIANS 4:23

Greatness

Large amount; extent

Our view of God, ourselves, and His plan for us is often too small. God wants us to come out of smallness and see the greatness of His calling and our inheritance in Him.

When we inherit a thing it means that we get what someone else worked for. Jesus gained a prize for us. He worked for what we inherit, and all He wants us to do is receive it by faith.

We don't have to wait for God to do something, because He has already done all that needs to be done. One step of faith will put you in the middle of relationship with God through Christ, and you can receive the greatest inheritance ever passed from one person to another. God has invited you to live a wonderful life. As 1 John 4:17 says, even "as He is, so are we in this world." That is good news!

> *In this [union and communion with Him]*
> *love is brought to completion and attains*
> *perfection with us… because as He is, so are*
> *we in this world.*   1 JOHN 4:17

History

An account of facts, particularly of facts respecting nations or states

---

While any history book is simply an account of what has happened in the past, the Bible is a history book of *God's* story, and He warned that no one should add to it or take away from it. History is really *His-story*.

If we don't pass the true story of God down to the next generation, it will be tragic. Only truth can keep people free, so tell your children and grandchildren everything you can about God. Tell them Bible stories and help them remember the great things that God has done.

Make sure that when you celebrate holidays like Christmas, Easter, and Thanksgiving that you use them as an opportunity to teach the next generation and remind yourself what they are truly about. History is informational, but *His-story* is transformational. Never forget what is really important.

> *You shall teach them diligently to your children . . . and shall speak of them when you sit in your house.*
>
> DEUTERONOMY 6:7 (AMP)

Risk

To venture; to dare to undertake

I believe we should live our lives with an enormous spirit of adventure and risk. We only get one trip through life, and I don't want to be old and have nothing but regrets.

We always face the struggle between faith and fear. Don't give in to fear of the unknown or of being adventurous—move past it and follow what God places on your heart to do. There will always be critics who tell us our faith is too risky, but don't let them cause you to live a small, boring life. You can fully live today by not giving in to fear, or by worrying about tomorrow.

If you step up to the plate, you might strike out, but if you don't try, you will never know the joy of hitting a home run.

It has been decided by us...to select men and send them to you with our beloved Barnabas and Paul, men who have risked their lives for the name of our Lord Jesus Christ.

ACTS 15:25–26 (AMP)

Bless

To pronounce a wish of happiness to one; to express a wish or desire of happiness

---

Jesus tells us to bless those who hurt us (see Matthew 5:44), but how do we do that? One way is by not speaking negatively about them or telling others what they did to us.

I believe we invite trouble into our lives when somebody does something wrong or hurtful to us and we tell other people about it for no reason except to gossip. When we are hurting, we want sympathy, we want people to know who hurt us and how it happened, but God does not want us to respond that way.

God wants us to trust Him to bring justice in our lives, and while we are waiting, to refuse to speak ill of others, to pray for them, and bless them. This is one important way we overcome evil with good (see Romans 12:21).

Bless those who persecute you [who are cruel in their attitude toward you]; bless and do not curse them.   ROMANS 12:14

Conviction

The act of convincing, or compelling one to admit the truth of a charge; the act of convincing of sin or sinfulness

―――――――

We all make mistakes—that is true. But equally true is the fact that most of us really *hate* making mistakes, doing wrong things, or causing problems. Many times the guilt we feel over our mistakes is much worse than the mistakes themselves.

We should, of course, be sorry, and we should always repent—which means we turn away from the sin and begin doing what is right, with God's help—but we are not supposed to hate or reject ourselves when we sin.

The Holy Spirit will bring conviction when we do something wrong, but He never brings condemnation. We can receive the forgiveness God freely offers and go on with our lives, constantly seeking to know God more. Conviction leads us to God to ask for forgiveness; condemnation pulls us away from Him in shame.

And when He comes, He will convict and convince the world and bring demonstration to it about sin and about righteousness (uprightness of heart and right standing with God) and about judgment.   JOHN 16:8

Choice

The voluntary act of selecting or separating from two or more things that which is preferred

---

Making right choices is very important because life is made up of a series of choices. Sometimes we like to blame everything on the devil, but the devil cannot run our lives if we are diligent about being obedient to God.

We will have strong emotions and feelings about a variety of things in life, but we must learn not to bow down to them and obey them if they are contrary to God's Word or His direction in our lives. We can choose to say no to our feelings and yes to God's instruction.

The Bible says God has set before us life and death, the blessings and the curses; therefore, choose life (see Deuteronomy 30:19). It's like a multiple-choice test with the answers right in front of us. The options are (a) Life or (b) Death. We don't even have to try to figure this one out. Choose life.

Listen obediently and pay attention to My commandments . . . to love the Lord your God and to serve Him with all your heart and with all your soul [your choices, your thoughts, your whole being].

DEUTERONOMY 11:13 (AMP)

Set

To solidify

———————

"Setting" your mind is probably one of the greatest and most beneficial things you can learn to do. To "set" your mind means to make up your mind firmly.

Wet concrete can be easily moved and is impressionable before it dries or sets. But once it does set, it is in place for good. It cannot be easily molded or changed.

The same principle applies to setting your mind. To set your mind is to determine decisively what you think, what you believe, and what you will or will not do— and to set it in such a way that you cannot be easily swayed or persuaded otherwise.

When you set your mind ahead of time, this is the best way to resist any temptation you might face in the heat of the moment. A mind that is set is a mind that stands firm.

And set your minds and keep them set on
what is above (the higher things), not on the
things that are on the earth.

COLOSSIANS 3:2

Keep

To preserve; to retain

In the previous devotional we talked about "setting" your mind, but once you've set your mind, it is important that you *keep* it set and not allow outside forces to reshape your thinking over time.

Make up your mind that you are going to keep it set on God and you are going to follow Him wholeheartedly, never giving up. Some people spend their entire lives starting and quitting. They never follow through with anything. They may set their mind, but when temptation comes, or when things get difficult, they don't keep it set.

I strongly encourage you to be someone who finishes what you start by keeping your mind set in the right direction all the way through to victory.

And set your minds and keep them set on what is above (the higher things), not on the things that are on the earth.

COLOSSIANS 3:2

Companion

One who keeps company with another; one with whom a person frequently associates, and converses

---

God is always with us. This truth makes all the difference in life and is the key to being able to live without fear.

If we are confident that God is with us, what do we have to fear? David was able to face Goliath because he knew God was with him. He did not rely on his own ability; he trusted God. We may not always know exactly what God is going to do, but we can relax, knowing that He will do what needs to be done at the right time.

We can easily feel afraid if we think about the future and all the things that are unknown to us. We can look at it two ways: We can either be negative and fearful, or we can be excited about being part of God's mystery, knowing He knows exactly what's going to happen and is right there with us, helping us and directing us.

Yes, though I walk through the [deep, sunless] valley of the shadow of death, I will fear or dread no evil, for You are with me.

PSALM 23:4

Believing

The cognitive process that leads to convictions

Believing the best of people is very helpful in the process of forgiving people who hurt or offend us. As human beings, we tend to be suspicious of others, and we often get hurt due to our own imagination. It is possible to believe someone hurt you on purpose when the truth is they were not even aware they hurt you at all.

There are still times when people hurt my feelings, but then I remember that I can choose whether to be hurt or to get over it. I can go through my day believing the best or believing the worst, so why not believe the best and enjoy my day?

I encourage you to be a person who believes the best about others. When you do, it will keep offense and bitterness out of your life and help you stay peaceful and joyful.

Love bears up under anything and everything that comes, is ever ready to believe the best of every person.   1 CORINTHIANS 13:7

Generous

Giving freely

We are never more like God than when we are helping others, showing His love to those who are hurting. If you are willing to share with others and meet their needs, God will not only meet your needs but He will give you an abundance of supply so you will always be able to give.

I encourage you to develop the mindset that you are a generous giver. Look for ways to give and for needy people to whom you can give. The more you reach out to others, the happier you will be.

Jesus said that we would always have the poor with us (see Matthew 26:11), and the Bible has more than two thousand Scriptures that deal with our responsibility to the poor and needy. Study what the Bible says about God's provision and see yourself as one who meets needs rather than one who is needy.

The generous man [is a source of blessing and] shall be prosperous and enriched, and he who waters will himself be watered [reaping the generosity he has sown].

PROVERBS 11:25 (AMP)

Obedience

Words or actions denoting submission to authority; dutifulness

---

God tells us to obey Him and we will be blessed. It sounds easy enough, so why do so many fail to do it? Because like children, we are often stubborn and want our own way even though our way is less than God's best.

Just like children, it is important for us to learn the discipline of obedience—and as we're learning, we can thank God for being patient. He sticks with us all the way through our childish attempts at getting our own way and believes in us even when we have a difficult time believing in ourselves.

God has a great plan for your life, but it is only possible if you'll obey His Word and follow His guidance. Keep learning and growing and you will eventually enjoy the fullness of all God intended for you.

If you are willing and obedient, you shall eat the good of the land.   ISAIAH 1:19

Healed

Restored to a sound state

_____

For many years the emotional wounds from being rejected during my childhood prevented me from responding properly in relationships, but Jesus healed me. And if you need emotional healing, He will heal you also. He gives us beauty for ashes (see Isaiah 61:3).

Years of emotional ups and downs can place so much stress on our systems that it ends up making us sick. Thankfully, Jesus is our Healer, and He can heal you everywhere you hurt.

God did not intend for us to be fearful and to hide from life; He has given us what we need to live life boldly and fully. If you feel you need emotional healing, I encourage you to realize Jesus can heal you emotionally the same as He can spiritually. He cares about every part of your being and intends for you to be whole and complete.

Heal me, O Lord, and I shall be healed;
save me, and I shall be saved, for You are my
praise.   JEREMIAH 17:14

Stable

Steady in purpose; constant; firm in resolution; not fickle or wavering

---

Many people struggle with emotional instability and believe it defines who they are. But your emotions are not who you are—they are how you feel. You are a spirit, you have a soul, and you live in a body. Your emotions are part of your soul. They belong to you; you don't belong to them. Learn to stand back and look at your emotional responses as something that belongs to you and over which you have control.

Do you dislike the feeling of watching yourself do and say things you know are ridiculous, but you seem to have no power to control yourself? The good news is God can help you to change if you're willing to trust Him and do whatever you need to do to change.

Start by believing you can be a mature, stable individual. God "is no respecter of persons" (Acts 10:34); what He does for one, He will do for another. He has taught me, as well as many others, to be a joyful, stable person, and He can do the same for you if you truly desire it.

The [uncompromisingly] righteous shall flourish like the palm tree... they shall grow like a cedar in Lebanon [majestic, stable, durable, and incorruptible]. PSALM 92:12

Test

That with which any thing is compared for proof of its genuineness; a standard

---

Have you ever gone to the furniture store to buy a chair without sitting on it? Have you ever purchased a car without test-driving it? Of course not, and God also tests us to reveal the quality of our faith.

No matter what we think of ourselves, we find out what we are truly like in times of difficulty. Good times don't bring out the worst in us, but hard times do. That's why God says these difficult times can actually be good for us. They allow us to see what is in our character that needs to be changed.

As we choose to learn to trust God during challenging times instead of getting upset, we experience His faithfulness, which, in turn, increases our faith for the next time we need it. The more we use our muscles, the more they grow—it's the same way with our faith in God.

Oh, let the wickedness of the wicked come to an end, but establish the just; for the righteous God tests the hearts and minds.　　PSALM 7:9 (NKJV)

Extra

**Beyond what is due, expected, or
necessary; additional**

We are all different, and we each have different needs. I urge you to go the extra
mile and begin to truly listen to what people tell you about their needs, being ready
to help them. Because sometimes we give
people what is easy for us to give, but we
are still not meeting their need.

Perhaps you can easily give people
words of encouragement, so you tend to
encourage everyone. This is good because
everyone needs some words of encouragement, but you might be giving those words
to people who really need you to see that,

more than words of encouragement, they need practical help in some way.

They may be three months behind on the rent and instead of simply encouraging them to believe God will provide, they need you to help them pay the rent. If you are not able to help financially, that is understandable, but it is good to at least consider doing something extra to go along with your words when the situation calls for more action.

But if anyone has this world's goods (resources for sustaining life) and sees his brother and fellow believer in need, yet closes his heart of compassion against him, how can the love of God live and remain in him?   1 JOHN 3:17

Resting

Ceasing to move or act; ceasing to be moved or agitated; lying; leaning; standing

Faith allows us to rest mentally and emotionally. Even our will gets a rest when we have faith in God. We don't worry or reason, we are not upset or downcast, and we are not trying to make something happen that is not God's will—we are resting.

Many people in the Bible had serious problems and yet they seemed to be peaceful. For example: Paul sang in jail. Jesus prayed for others while being crucified. Joseph decided that if he was going to be a prisoner (even though he did not commit a crime) that he would be a prisoner with a good attitude.

We need to be honest about what the real cause of our stress is. Is it really our circumstances in life, or is it the way we respond to the circumstances? Entering the rest of God should be a priority for us because it is the only way we can truly enjoy our life.

And the Lord said, My Presence shall go with you, and I will give you rest.   EXODUS 33:14

Blessed

**Made happy or prosperous;
extolled; pronounced happy**

God is always good, and as His children, we have many blessings to be thankful for. For example...

If you woke up this morning with more body parts that don't hurt than those that do, you are blessed.

If you have food, clothes, and a place to live, you are richer than seventy-five percent of the world.

If you have money in the bank, in your wallet, or spare change at home, you are among the top 8 percent of the world's wealthiest people.

If you have never experienced the danger of battle, the loneliness of imprisonment, the agony of torture, or the pangs of starvation, you are ahead of five hundred million people in the world.

If you can read this devotional, you are more blessed than two billion people in the world who cannot read.

Spend some time today thanking God for all of your blessings.

O taste and see that the Lord [our God] is good; how blessed [fortunate, prosperous, and favored by God] is the man who takes refuge in Him. PSALM 34:8 (AMP)

Disconnect

To separate; to disunite

We need safe people in our lives, not ones who are volatile and are merely bombs waiting to explode. We need people who add to our lives, not ones who drain us. That's why sometimes the best thing we can do is disconnect from an unhealthy friendship.

Some people think that holding on is heroic, but sometimes disconnecting is the most heroic thing we can do. This is an area in which we must learn to be led by the Holy Spirit. I don't advocate giving up on people easily; however, if the relationship is making you sick emotionally and draining you of the energy you need for your life, then disconnecting may be the only thing you can do.

Sometimes letting go is just a decision to stop trying to change them, and at other times it requires walking away. Walking away is not easy, but there are times in life when we must do it. Remember that God will always give you the grace to do what you need to do in life through Christ (see Philippians 4:13).

> *Do not be so deceived and misled! Evil companionships (communion, associations) corrupt and deprave good manners and morals and character.*   1 CORINTHIANS 15:33

Resist

Literally, to stand against; to withstand; hence, to act in opposition or to oppose

---

Satan wants our joy because it is our strength (see Nehemiah 8:10). He attacks with fear in order to steal the joy that Jesus has provided for us. He also uses the same tactic to try to steal our peace.

God's Word instructs us to "watch and pray" (see Matthew 26:41), and it is good advice. Watch your thoughts, pay attention to what your emotions are doing, how you're feeling, and what decisions you are making. If you are sensing the beginning of anything that seems the least bit ungodly or that will diminish you in any way, pray immediately and resist the temptation in the power of God.

Satan looks for weaknesses that he can take advantage of, and we should be watching for his attacks, so we can resist at the onset of them and defeat him every time.

So be subject to God. Resist the devil [stand firm against him], and he will flee from you.

JAMES 4:7

Ability

Physical power, whether bodily or mental; natural or acquired; force of understanding; skill in arts or science

---

The world is filled with dissatisfied, unfulfilled people, and I suspect it is because they are not giving themselves to what they were meant to do.

God has given each of us gifts and abilities, and we should nurture and develop them. Paul wrote to the Romans telling them to give themselves to whatever their gift was (see Romans 12:6–8).

I am gifted as a public speaker, but I am not gifted as a musician. I tried in the earlier years of my life to learn to play the guitar, but it was a waste of time. We cannot accomplish a thing merely because we want to do so. God helps us do only what He wants us to do. Find out what that means for you and give yourself to it wholeheartedly.

But offer yourselves to God... [all of your abilities—sanctified, set apart] as instruments of righteousness [yielded] to God.

ROMANS 6:13 (AMP)

Plan

A project; the form of something to be done existing in the mind, with the several parts adjusted in idea, expressed in words, or committed to writing

---

I used to get very discouraged when my plans didn't work out or I didn't reach my goals, but I finally realized that if I truly want to serve God with my life, it shouldn't matter what I am doing, as long as it is His plan for me.

Perhaps we have too many of our own plans, and it is our own expectations that disappoint us. We can and should pray as

Jesus prayed, "Your will be done, oh, God, and not Mine."

You may feel that you don't know what God's will is, but you can easily find it if you pay attention to what you are good at, what you enjoy and feel at ease with. Don't be afraid to try things and keep on trying until you find what fits.

Father, if You are willing, remove this cup from Me; yet not My will, but [always] Yours be done.   LUKE 22:42

Unconditionally

**Without terms of limitation;
without reservation**

"What is wrong with me?" If you are like most people, you have asked yourself that question many times throughout your life. I know I asked myself that for many years and it's a common question the enemy plants in people's minds. It is designed to make you feel as if you are not what you need to be and to prevent you from enjoying life.

There is, however, an antidote for this type of thinking that poisons our lives. It is thinking frequently, *God loves me uncon-ditionally, and He is not keeping a list of my faults!* Not only does God love us but He chooses to view us as being right with Him, accepted and blameless through the blood of Christ.

This confidence can be ours through our faith in Jesus Christ and through believing God's Word. You are the righteousness of God in Christ, and You are loved unconditionally!

> *Nor height nor depth, nor anything else in all creation will be able to separate us from the love of God which is in Christ Jesus our Lord.*   ROMANS 8:39

Content

Satisfied

_____

I have seen people who, at the end of their lives, had only regret about the way they had lived and felt no satisfaction and contentment. But I think it is beautiful to see an elderly person who says, "My life has been good. When it is time for me to die, I can die happy."

People who aren't content have never developed a habit of being appreciative and thankful. Honestly, just to be able to walk, see, and hear is a great blessing and one that people who are crippled, blind, or deaf would be extremely content with. If you were in the hospital, you would be content just to sit in your own home in your favorite chair.

We always think we will be content *when*... But why not choose to be content right now? Be content with what you have; refuse to focus on what you don't have.

> *Not that I am implying that I was in any personal want, for I have learned how to be content (satisfied to the point where I am not disturbed or disquieted) in whatever state I am.*   PHILIPPIANS 4:11

Difference

The quality that distinguishes one thing from another

In order to have good relationships, it is vital that we learn to accept the differences in all people. God created us all differently on purpose. Those who are different from you are not just people who got in all the wrong lines when God was passing out personality traits.

I have a friend who is so nice that I am surprised her name is not Sugar. I am working on it, but I doubt I will ever be as naturally nice as she is. I have thought, *Where was I when God handed out the "sweet personalities"?* I was right where I was supposed to be, getting what God wanted me to have, and so were you and everyone else.

Let's remember that God created each of us in our mother's womb carefully and intricately. There is nothing wrong with a person just because they're not like someone else.

I will give thanks and praise to You, for
I am fearfully and wonderfully made;
wonderful are Your works, and my soul
knows it very well.   PSALM 139:14 (AMP)

Self-Esteem

The esteem or opinion of oneself

Have you ever taken any time to consider what you think about yourself? Most people have not, but it is an important thing to do.

I can remember desperately struggling for many years with my self-esteem, but I finally learned to see myself as God does, and it revolutionized my life. My father had told me I was no good and would never amount to anything, but God tells me that I am His and that through Him, I can do greater things than I could ever imagine. And the same is true for you!

It really isn't what other people think

about us that hurts us; it is what we think of ourselves. This is why it is so important to view yourself through the viewpoint of God's Word. He created you, He has given you unique gifts and talents, and He loves you with an everlasting love.

> *So God created man in His own image, in the image and likeness of God He created him; male and female He created them.*
>
> GENESIS 1:27

Sanctified

Made holy; consecrated; set apart for sacred services

We are made right with God through faith in Christ. Then God, by His grace, changes us on the inside, and the Holy Spirit works with us, teaching us to live inside out! We are sanctified, and that means we are set apart and made holy by Him.

These and many other wonderful works are accomplished in our spirits by God's grace. It is His gift to us! When we learn to believe what God has done in us, we will produce the fruit of it in our daily lives.

We may not do everything right, but

God views us as right through our faith in Jesus and His work on the cross for us. This is the beauty of sanctification. Because of Jesus, we are clean and spotless in the eyes of our Heavenly Father, and as we continue walking with Him, our behavior becomes more and more like His.

Therefore Jesus also suffered and died outside the [city's] gate in order that He might purify and consecrate the people through [the shedding of] His own blood and set them apart as holy [for God].   HEBREWS 13:12

Unfamiliar

Not accustomed; not common; not rendered agreeable by frequent use

---

One of the obstacles to following God is uncertainty simply because, quite often, we have not passed this way before. Things that are unfamiliar—things we've never done before—naturally make us feel a little more timid than usual. God loves to lead us into new things!

People have asked me if I'm ever nervous or fearful, and my answer is yes. When I am doing something for the first time, something I am totally unfamiliar with, I am tempted to lose my confidence just like everyone else, but I choose to trust God and continue going forward.

My best advice is this: Press forward into what you believe God's will is for you. Don't let the feeling of uncertainty rule your decisions. Be diligent to apply God's Word to your life and stay close to Him. You may be unfamiliar with this new thing, but God isn't. He knows exactly where He is taking you and what He has planned for your life.

But He knows the way that I take [He has concern for it, appreciates, and pays attention to it].   JOB 23:10

Failure

**An event that does not accomplish
its intended purpose**

No one sets out to fail or enjoys failing.
But did you know that "failure" can be an
important stepping-stone on the way to
success? When we fail it teaches us what
not to do, which is often as important as
knowing what we *are* to do. Failure can
actually be a benefit.

There are many stories told about how
many times Thomas Edison tried and
failed before he successfully invented the
incandescent light bulb. I've heard he tried
seven hundred times, two thousand times,
and even ten thousand times. Whatever

the true number is, it's a staggering number of attempts. But Edison never gave up. It's reported that he said in all his efforts, he never failed—not once; he just had to go through many, many steps to get it right!

It takes that kind of determination to do anything worthwhile. Failure doesn't have to be the end; failure can be a new beginning.

For a righteous man falls seven times and rises again.   PROVERBS 24:16

Abandon

To resign; to yield, relinquish, or give over entirely

I believe one of the most freeing things you can do as a Christian is to abandon yourself to God, letting go of trying to control your life and circumstances and trusting Him with everything.

Abandonment is forgetting the past entirely, leaving the future in God's hands, and being totally at peace with the present, knowing that you are in God's perfect will for you for that moment.

Watchman Nee, a martyr for Christ, died with this note under his pillow: *"Christ is the Son of God. He died to atone for men's sin, and after three days rose again. This is the most important fact in the universe. I die believing in Christ."*

Watchman Nee had abandoned all to God. Nothing could stop him from trusting, not even impending death. If we can learn to have this kind of faith, we will do amazing things for God.

We too might walk habitually in newness of life [abandoning our old ways].

ROMANS 6:4 (AMP)

Excellent

Being of great value or use, applied to things; remarkable for good properties

---

It is very easy to be a mediocre person. All you have to do is make no extra effort and drift through life making no difference in the world, which will guarantee that you leave no legacy behind when you are gone.

But if you will dare to be an excellent person in all you do, you will be a bright light in the darkness, and that is exactly what God has called you to be.

God is excellent and we are created in His image; therefore, if we are to reach our full potential in Him, we must also choose to be excellent. God has an excellent plan for our lives, but a mediocre, compromising person will not live in the fulfillment of an excellent destiny.

We all have a choice to make about how we will live, and I believe God wants us to choose to always do our best for Him in order to walk in excellence.

Keep your behavior excellent among the [unsaved] Gentiles [conduct yourself honorably, with graciousness and integrity].

1 PETER 2:12 (AMP)

Margin

A measure, quantity, or degree of difference

Do you use your time wisely, or are you stressed-out by an overly busy, hectic schedule frequently? If you find yourself rushed and always in a hurry, you will probably need to locate the root of your problem. Hurry may just be a bad habit, but it can also be the fruit of procrastination. People who procrastinate, who don't take action when they should, will ultimately be in a hurry.

I encourage you to learn to live with margin. That means you allocate more time to get ready to do things and get places than you think you might need. Then, if something happens that you didn't expect to happen, you will be prepared.

I have learned through experiencing many frustrating days that the best plan is to leave margin for the unexpected things. In other words, I have learned to expect the unexpected. Declare war on hurry, and stay in the battle until you have detected and defeated every enemy of your peace.

Therefore see that you walk carefully...
making the very most of your time [on earth,
recognizing and taking advantage of each
opportunity and using it with wisdom and
diligence].   EPHESIANS 5:15–16 (AMP)

Responsible

Accountable; answerable; amenable

Everyone who is successful is also responsible. Success and personal responsibility cannot be separated.

It doesn't matter how many opportunities we have in life, we won't accomplish them successfully if we aren't responsible to do what we need to do to take advantage of them. I boldly ask you to examine your life truthfully. Are you a responsible individual? Are there areas in which you could improve? Do you make excuses when you do something wrong? As I often say, facing truth is often emotionally painful, but it is one of the most powerful and freeing things we can do.

Responsible people cease asking themselves how they *feel* early in life because they know there will be times when they won't feel like doing what they should be doing, but they do it anyway. I encourage you to embrace new levels of personal responsibility in order to experience new levels of success.

So then, each of us will give an account of himself to God. ROMANS 14:12 (AMP)

Outlook

The point of view or attitude of a person

There once was a woman who woke up one morning, looked in the mirror, and noticed she had only three hairs on her head. "Well," she said, "I think I'll braid my hair today." So she did, and she had a great day. The next day she woke up, looked in the mirror, and saw she had only two hairs on her head. "Hmmm," she said, "I think I'll part my hair down the middle today." So she did, and she had a grand day. The next day she woke up, looked in the mirror, and noticed that she had only one hair on her head. "Well," she said, "today

I'm going to wear my hair in a ponytail." So she did, and she had a fun, fun day. The next day she woke up, looked in the mirror, and noticed that there wasn't a single hair on her head. "Yay!" she exclaimed. "I don't have to fix my hair today!"

This little story shows us a woman who was determined to have a positive, joy-filled outlook on life. Wouldn't our lives be so much better if we followed her example?

Be happy [in your faith] and rejoice and be glad-hearted continually (always).

1 THESSALONIANS 5:16

Enjoy

To feel or perceive with pleasure

God wants us to enjoy our lives in christ. So each day we need to encourage ourselves yourself with the promises from God's Word, such as:

- No condemnation is from the Lord. Live in the power of grace.
- Joy is for the journey. Choose to be joyful regardless of your circumstances.
- Obey when the Lord speaks to you.
- Yesterday is over. Refuse to live in the past.

- Live by faith, not feelings.
- Invite Christ into every area of your life.
- Forgive those who hurt you.
- Expect God's goodness in every situation.

I came that they may have and enjoy life, and have it in abundance (to the full, till it overflows).　　　JOHN 10:10

Position

Manner of standing or being placed; attitude

You've been given a powerful new position in Christ. Don't let the devil tell you that you are anything less than the amazing person God has created you to be.

You are a joint heir with Christ, loved and approved by God Himself. Spend each day in the confidence of your position in Christ. It is this assurance that will inspire you to make God-honoring choices in your life and to begin pursuing God with a renewed passion.

In my years spent studying and teaching God's Word, I've discovered this important truth: It is never too late to discover your true identity. Whatever you've been through, God wants you to understand the position you have as His son or daughter. You have more value than you could possibly know.

Let the brother in humble circumstances glory in his high position [as a born-again believer, called to the true riches and to be an heir of God].   JAMES 1:9 (AMP)

Celebrate

To praise; to extol; to commend; to give to; to make famous; as, to *celebrate* the name of the Most High

---

You have much to celebrate today as a believer in Jesus Christ. Joy and peace can be yours. You are redeemed, accepted, and made right with God today—not someday, but today!

The truth is, we don't really need more things in order to be happy; we simply need to celebrate what we already have in Christ and what God has already done. When we truly know God and see the hope of His calling and our inheritance in

Christ, we will celebrate His goodness and be an example for others to follow.

When you live out of a place of gratitude and celebration, you will discover the power of God in your life. No obstacle, situation, or adversary will be able to stop you from enjoying your life and accomplishing much for the Kingdom of God. You will live in the spirit of celebration because of what you know in your heart to be true.

And David and all Israel merrily celebrated before God with all their might, with songs and lyres and harps and tambourines and cymbals and trumpets.

1 CHRONICLES 13:8

Vacation

Leisure; freedom from trouble or perplexity

When we learn to live without worrying, we can do our work, or whatever else we need to do on a regular basis, all the while with our soul on vacation. That is what it means to take refuge in God. He is our resting place. We can deal with circumstances that are unpleasant and handle all the responsibility we have, and yet remain totally peaceful and calm.

I recall sharing this message once in a church, and the pastor of the church got a revelation of what I was saying and literally threw his hands up in the air, slid down into a relaxed position in his seat, and said, "I can pastor this church while my soul is on vacation."

Whatever your assignment is in life, you can enjoy the entire process if you learn how to let your soul (mind, will, and emotions) rest in God. Even though there may be busyness on the outside, your soul can be on vacation through it all as you lean on and trust in God.

Be merciful and gracious to me, O God, be merciful and gracious to me, for my soul takes refuge and finds shelter and confidence in You.   PSALM 57:1

Refuse

To decline to accept what is offered; as, to refuse an office; to refuse an offer

---

When people hurt or offend you, you may not be able to help the way you feel, but you can help what you do about it. You can turn the entire situation over to God and refuse to be offended.

I heard a story about a pastor I know: He was hosting a guest speaker in his church, and the guest made critical remarks about the way the church handled its services. The guest speaker was young and inexperienced, and the pastor refused to let the comments offend him. He sat in the front row and repeated in a low whisper, "I will not get offended. I will not get offended."

This story has stuck with me for a long time because it is an excellent example of someone who took action to make sure no root of offense or bitterness got into his heart. He believed the best and refused the worst.

But I tell you, Love your enemies and pray for those who persecute you.   MATTHEW 5:44

Truth

Veracity; purity from falsehood

God's Word is truth, and when we love it and obey it, we are set free from bondages that have held us captive. Don't ever be afraid of truth. It brings light into your life and dispels darkness.

Embrace the light of God's truth. Yes, it is a little difficult to look at the light if one has been in the dark a long time, but we adjust quickly and realize it is much better to live in the light than it is to live in the darkness.

The Holy Spirit consistently teaches us and reveals the truth to us. It is an ongoing process in our lives and one that can and should be exciting. He shows us what is wrong because He wants to deliver us and make our lives better. In order to do that, we must see and accept the truth, be sorry for our sins, and be willing to turn away from the dark to the light.

Sanctify them [purify, consecrate, separate them for Yourself, make them holy] by the Truth; Your Word is Truth.   JOHN 17:17

Listen

To hearken; to give ear; to attend closely with a view to hear

---

In order for us to walk in love with others the way Jesus loves us, we must overcome a selfish, self-centered mind-set and approach to life. One of the best ways to wage a war on selfishness is to realize that people are different and they need different things. Therefore, we can start training ourselves to really listen to what they tell us.

I have found that if I listen to anyone for very long, I can walk away with a pretty specific knowledge of something I can get for them, do for them, or pray about for them if I really want to.

The "I don't know what to do" excuse is an old one and needs to be put in the trash. If we really want to love others, we can find ways to do it. It all begins with being attentive, listening carefully, and looking for ways to bless the people in our lives. Remember, indifference makes excuses, but love finds a way.

Understand [this], my beloved brethren. Let every man be quick to hear [a ready listener], slow to speak, slow to take offense and to get angry.   JAMES 1:19

Adventurous

Inclined or willing to incur hazard; bold to encounter danger; daring; courageous; enterprising

---

Every human being wants to be free. We want to try new things, to be bold and fearless, to live an exciting, adventurous life.

We were created by God to have goals and to press toward them, and to dream of bigger and better things than what we have ever known. But fear and doubt can leave us frozen in place, unable to do much of anything except be idle and alone with our torment. As long as we become inactive every time we feel a doubt or have a sense of worry, we won't live in confidence and we'll miss out on the exciting, adventurous life God has for us.

Please be assured that Jesus died not only for the forgiveness of your sins but also so that you might enjoy a passionate, fruitful, and powerful life in Him. Be determined to experience all that He died to give you.

I am . . . being ardent and passionate for God just as all of you are today.   ACTS 22:3 (AMP)

Equal

**Just; equitable; giving the same or
similar rights or advantages**

The world places labels and assigns vary-
ing values to almost everything, but in
God's eyes, we are all equal. He loves and
values each of us equally. We are all one in
Christ!

Don't spend your time thinking over
and over about your faults. And don't compare yourself with other people, thinking that you should strive to be like them.
Oscar Wilde said, "Be yourself; everyone
else is already taken."

I strongly suggest that you make peace
with yourself, if you haven't already done

so, and learn to think about yourself the way God does. Remember, God loves you just as much as He does everyone else. We are all equal in His sight.

> *There is no [distinction between] Greek and Jew, circumcised and uncircumcised, [nor between nations whether] barbarian or Scythian, [nor in status whether] slave or free, but Christ is all, and in all [so believers are equal in Christ, without distinction].*
>
> COLOSSIANS 3:11 (AMP)

Stretched

Extended; exerted to the utmost

When you follow God into something new in your life, you may feel stretched.

Perhaps you receive a job promotion, and you know you don't have all the natural skills and knowledge you need to do the new job well. Then you become worried because you think you're in over your head. The job may be over your head, but it's not bigger than God. If He leads you into it, He will help you fulfill the responsibilities that go with it. God's power and presence enable us to do things we can't do on our own.

It's important to remember God is on

your side as you go into new situations, because fear and doubt will always be lying in wait to try to keep you from following Him. Don't let those things hold you back. Remember that God is with you and He's bigger than any problem you may face. Don't be afraid to stretch your faith because it will give you greater capacity to fulfill your God-given potential.

For we walk by faith . . . not by sight or appearance.   2 CORINTHIANS 5:7

Forethought

A thinking beforehand; anticipation; prescience; premeditation

_____

Before you make any commitment—even a small one—ask yourself if you truly believe you can and will actually follow through with it.

Some people set unrealistic goals and they always fail. A little bit of forethought could have saved them lots of trouble and frustration. Be realistic about how long it takes to do things, and allow yourself enough time to do them without being stressed-out about them.

If you need to say no to a request, don't

hesitate to do so. We are responsible to follow God's expectations of us, not everyone else's. If you'll take time to think ahead before committing yourself to things, you'll be surprised at how much time, energy, and peace of mind you will save in the long run.

For which of you, wishing to build a farm
building, does not first sit down and calculate
the cost [to see] whether he has sufficient
means to finish it? LUKE 14:28

Step

To go; to walk a little distance

Today, I want to encourage you to do whatever God leads you to do. You may not have all the answers, and you may not know every step to take, but by faith you can take the first step. Maybe that step is:

- Applying for a class at your local community college
- Forgiving the person you've held a grudge against
- Going to church for the first time in years
- Making an appointment with a nutritionist

- Sending out a résumé
- Calling an adoption agency
- Praying a bold prayer, asking God for what seems impossible

You've waited, grieved, or made excuses long enough. Now it's time to believe. Take a step and watch what God can do!

For [God's] eyes are upon the ways of a man, and He sees all his steps.   JOB 34:21

Ask

To request; to seek to obtain by words; to petition

God surely knew that we would all need help in life because He sent us His Holy Spirit Who is referred to as the Helper. One of the best prayers we can pray is: "Lord, I need help!" Asking is the first rule to receiving, so don't be too prideful to ask for help.

Isaiah said that all people grow weary at times. No matter what our age is or how naturally strong we are, we all have limits and that is okay. It is okay if you cannot do it all. In fact, you can't do it all. Isaiah's instruction was to wait upon the Lord and be refreshed and renewed (see Isaiah 40:-28–31).

Isaiah knew what many other people in the Bible also knew—David, Ruth, Gideon, Mary, Peter, and Paul (to name a few). He knew that asking for help is a sign of wisdom, not of weakness. Not only is it okay to ask for help, it is essential that we do so on a regular basis.

You do not have, because you do not ask.

JAMES 4:2

Consecrated

Separated from a common to a sacred use; devoted or dedicated to the service and worship of God

---

God is pleased with us as His children. He loves and accepts us as we are, and if our hearts are right toward Him, then we will also want to please Him in all things—how we dress, how we spend our money, what our entertainment choices are, what we read, watch, and talk about.

It is true that God loves us no matter what choice we make, but He also said that if we love Him, we will obey Him (see John 14:15). Total consecration takes time and is definitely a lifelong journey. The question is, where are you headed? I trust that you want God's will more than anything and that you are willing to be obedient to Him in every area of your life.

When we give our all to God, when we obey Him in all things, and when we want only what He wants us to have, it is then that we can really celebrate and enjoy the life Jesus came to give us.

Therefore you are no longer outsiders . . . but you now share citizenship with the saints (God's own people, consecrated and set apart for Himself). EPHESIANS 2:19

Self-Discipline

Correction or government of one's self for the sake of improvement

How do you view self-discipline? Do you see it as something that controls you, or something that helps you control yourself? Do you see it as something you have to do, or something that helps you become the person you truly want to be? Living a disciplined life is the only pathway to freedom.

- Disciplining ourselves to exercise and develop good eating habits sets us free to feel good and be comfortable in our clothes.

- Disciplining ourselves to manage our money wisely sets us free from the pressure of need and debt.
- Disciplining ourselves to be excellent rather than mediocre or lazy gives us the enjoyment of self-respect.

Self-discipline is hard work, but it is easier than trying to live a life that is out of control.

He who has no rule over his own spirit is like a city that is broken down and without walls.   PROVERBS 25:28

Knowing

**Having clear and certain
perception of**

There is a big difference between knowing *about* God and knowing God. When
we truly know God, we also experience
(know) His power.

The apostle Paul was determined to
know God and the power of His resurrection, and he understood that achieving
his goal would be a lifelong pursuit. He
knew that attaining this knowledge and
relationship with God was not something
he could get by reasoning or from book
learning alone, but it had to be sought

diligently and would be acquired progressively throughout his life (see Philippians 3:10).

As we are hungry for a deeper relationship with God and we are diligent in seeking Him, He reveals Himself to us in a very personal way. This deep, intimate knowledge enables us to remain stable and firm in faith even during very difficult times.

I want to know Christ and experience the
mighty power that raised him from the dead.

PHILIPPIANS 3:10 (NLT)

Confront

**To stand face-to-face in full view;
to face; to stand in front of**

Sometimes in life we are confronted with problems that we did not expect. When that happens it is important that we confront them and that we never run away. We cannot escape trouble by ignoring it or running from it.

Anytime we run from a situation, we will likely have to go back and face it, or something very similar, at a later time in our lives. Think about Moses. He ran from Egypt and spent forty years in the desert, where God prepared him to be a great leader. When God appeared to him in the burning bush, He basically said: "Okay, now I want you to go back to Egypt" (see Exodus 3:2–10). Yes, God sent Moses right back to the place he tried to escape from.

If you want to live an overcoming life, ask God to help you have the boldness to confront any problem and deal with it in His strength.

They confronted and came upon me in the day of my calamity, but the Lord was my stay and support.   PSALM 18:18

Level

A certain position, rank, standard, degree, quality, character, etc.

We never stay in the same place in life, merely remaining static; we are always stepping into new levels. We do things we have never done before and face new responsibilities. We are presented with new opportunities, and many times they come with new opposition.

We have an enemy, the devil and he does not want us to make any kind of positive progress in life. The apostle Paul said in I Corinthians 16:9 that a wide door of opportunity had opened unto him and with it came many adversaries.

If God has promoted you to a new level of something or given you a new opportunity, you can be assured that He will guide and strengthen you for the challenge. When opposition comes stand firm and be full of confidence because God is with you and you are more than a conqueror (see Romans 8:37).

He Who began a good work in you will
continue until the day of Jesus Christ...
perfecting and bringing it to full completion
in you.   PHILIPPIANS 1:6

Happy

Feeling pleasure; content

———————

What would you say if I told you we have an obligation to be as happy as we can possibly be? I believe we glorify God the most when we are the happiest in Him. Look at Psalm 37:4 again: it says we are to delight ourselves "in the Lord."

I have striven for many years to learn how to do just that. Because of the way I was raised, I had the idea it was wrong to enjoy myself, until I saw that Jesus said He came so we might have joy in our lives and have it in abundance (see John 10:10, 16:24, 17:13). He wants our joy to be full!

The belief that holiness and happiness

are at odds with each other is tragic. Let me assure you that you can live a life that is holy and pleasing to God and thoroughly enjoy your life at the same time. Smile, laugh, be happy and enjoy each moment that God gives you while you serve Him with your whole heart.

Delight yourself also in the Lord, and He will give you the desires and secret petitions of your heart.   PSALM 37:4

Vindicator

**One who justifies or maintains;
one who defends**

God has promised to be our Vindicator. He brings justice into our lives and makes wrong things right if we trust Him.

I was a victim of sexual abuse as a child, and for many years I was very angry. I was so filled with anger it came out of me in situations and toward people that had nothing to do with the pain of my past. I felt I was owed something and I was trying to collect from the whole world. I finally realized nobody could pay me back for what my abuser took from me. That is, nobody but God. He has promised to give us a double recompense for our former trouble (see Isaiah 61:7), and I am living testimony of the faithfulness of God.

Don't spend your life trying to collect past debts from people who have no ability or intention to pay. Let God be your Vindicator.

For I know that my Redeemer and Vindicator lives, and at last He [the Last One] will stand upon the earth.   JOB 19:25

Quality

Having a high degree of excellence

Quality is much more important than quantity. It is rare to find a person who gives his whole heart to what he is doing and strives to do it with excellence.

The world and our culture are rapidly changing but something that society is always looking for is someone who produces quality work and lives a life of excellence in every area.

We desperately need Christians who will take a stand, who will say, "I will dare to live with purpose and passion. I will dare to live with excellence and commitment. I will do my very best to be the best me I can be. I will have the courage to be one of the few!"

Will you be one of those people? Will you strive to do your best in order to live a life of quality and excellence today?

See what [an incredible] quality of love the Father has given (shown, bestowed on) us, that we should [be permitted to] be named and called and counted the children of God!

1 JOHN 3:1

Motivate

**To provide with an incentive or a
reason for doing something; impel**

Why you do a thing is just as important (if
not more so) than *what* you do. Motives
matter! Here are some good motivators to
have in your life:

- The Word of God—Being obedient
  to the Word of God is the best
  motivator I know of.
- Pure love—This motivator is
  important because Jesus said it
  is by love that the world would
  recognize us as His disciples (John
  13:34-35).

- Faith—Our faith pleases God
  (Hebrews 11:6); therefore, this
  motivator in life makes God smile.
- To be a blessing—Jesus went
  about doing good (Acts 10:35).
  Let's strive to be like Him!
- For the sake of righteousness—A
  good motivator is simply doing a
  thing because it is the right thing
  to do.

Keeping our motives pure is a lifelong
process, but one worth pursuing. Ask God
to help you have the right motives.

*Your work energized by faith and service
motivated by love and unwavering hope in
[the return of] our Lord Jesus Christ (the
Messiah)...*   1 THESSALONIANS 1:3

Cast

**To throw, fling, or send; that is, to
drive from, by force, as from the
hand, or from an engine**

Regrets and dreads are unhealthy, fear-
based cares that will drag you down and
keep you from new levels of victory in your
life. This is why they must be confronted.
If you're afraid of your past and afraid of
your future, you'll be frozen in a dysfunc-
tional present.

There is only one solution, and it comes
straight from the Word of God—cast your
cares upon the Lord. This has been one of
the most freeing things I've learned to do
as a Christian. Rather than regret the past

or dread the future, I just cast every care upon God and trust Him to give me peace. This allows me to fully enjoy the present.

I encourage you to do the same thing. God is a God of justice, and that means that He makes every wrong thing right if we trust Him to do so. God loves you and He delights in taking care of you and all your concerns.

Casting the whole of your care [all your anxieties, all your worries, all your concerns, once and for all] on Him, for He cares for you affectionately and cares about you watchfully.   1 PETER 5:7

Seed

That from which any thing springs; first principle; original

There is nothing too small to give to God. Each decision that you make for Him is a seed you sow that will reap a plentiful harvest.

You are making a bigger impact than you know. Don't devalue any seemingly little thing that you do or give. The little bit you have—time, talent, energy, offerings, and obedience—is more than enough in the hands of God.

Don't be discouraged or grow impatient. Living for God is rarely a huge, cataclysmic event. It is more of a disciplined, faithful, step-by-step process. But with the help of the Lord these seeds you are sowing are going to bring a harvest. All you have to do is stay faithful, keep planting, and refuse to give up.

See how the farmer waits expectantly for the precious harvest from the land. [See how] he keeps up his patient [vigil] over it until it receives the early and late rains.   JAMES 5:7

Difference

A noticeable change or effect

Adapted from Loren Eiseley's essay, "The Star Thrower," a story is told of a man who learned the value of one:

While wandering a deserted beach at dawn, stagnant in my work, I saw a man in the distance bending and throwing as he walked the endless stretch toward me. As he came near, I could see that he was throwing starfish, abandoned by the tide, back into the sea.

When he was close enough, I asked him why he was working so hard at this strange task. He said that the sun would dry the starfish and they would die. I told him he was foolish because there were thousands of starfish on miles of beach. One man alone could never make a difference. He smiled as he picked up the next starfish. Hurling it into the sea he said, "It makes a difference for this one."

Never underestimate the difference you can make, even if it's just for one person.

This is My commandment: that you love one another [just] as I have loved you.

JOHN 15:12

Redeem

To rescue; to recover; to deliver from

The Word of God tells us we can "exult and triumph in our troubles" (see Romans 5:3). I know it sounds counterintuitive to actually rejoice when you are facing a trouble, but when you know God is with you and you choose to stand in faith, knowing He has a great plan for your life, you understand that He can redeem any situation.

God can use a broken plan to produce something beautiful.

God wasn't surprised when your Plan A failed. He exists outside of time, and He knows the end from the beginning. He can redeem that failure or that struggle and use it to produce something good in your life.

When you go through something difficult, instead of spending your entire prayer time asking God to deliver you from it, I encourage you to stop and ask God to do something amazing in the midst of it.

Redeem Israel, O God, out of all their troubles.   PSALM 25:22

Sure

Certain; unfailing; infallible

Because of the promises in the Word of God, there are some things we can be sure of. Not maybe, not probably...we can be *sure* they are true.

- We can be sure we are children of God, and that we are loved, called, anointed, and appointed by Him.
- We can be sure that we have righteousness, peace, and joy in the Holy Spirit.
- We can be sure that we are forgiven for all of our sins and our

names are written in the Lamb's
Book of Life.

- We can be sure that we have been
  guaranteed an inheritance, for it
  was purchased with the blood of
  Jesus.
- We can be sure that Jesus has gone
  before us to prepare a place for us
  in heaven.

These promises (and many others) are
certainties that we can build our lives upon.
They are sure to be true!

*The works of His hands are [absolute]
truth and justice [faithful and right]; and
all His decrees and precepts are sure (fixed,
established, and trustworthy).*   PSALM 111:7

Powerful

Having great physical or mechanical power; strong; forcible; mighty

---

In the letter to the Ephesians, Paul prayed that we would know the exceeding greatness of God's power toward us. God is powerful and anyone who believes in God surely believes that, but the question is: Do we believe that His power is available to us and that it exists for us?

This is a power that has already been given. In Luke 10:19, Jesus said, "Behold! I have given you authority and power." We do not need to strive for power or hope to have power someday—we have power now!

The same power that raised Christ from the dead dwells in us (see Romans 8:11), and we can be quickened (filled with life) by that power. Through faith we can be daily filled, and we can enjoy His Presence at all times.

And [so that you can know and understand] what is the immeasurable and unlimited and surpassing greatness of His power in and for us who believe...   EPHESIANS 1:19

Reality

Actual being or existence of any thing; truth; fact; in distinction from mere appearance

---

I have adopted a new phrase, and it is helping me to deal with reality and not waste my time being upset about things I cannot do anything about. I have been saying, "It is what it is."

Somehow that is a reality check for me, and I quickly realize I need to deal with things the way they are, not the way I wish they were. It does no good to live in a false sense of reality. Whatever we have to deal with on a given day, we can do it with the help of God.

You are never going to have anyone else's life, so wanting it is unrealistic and a waste of time. Learn to thank God for the life He has given you and make the most of each day with a thankful heart.

A time will come, however, indeed it is already here, when the true (genuine) worshipers will worship the Father in spirit and in truth (reality); for the Father is seeking just such people as these as His worshipers.   JOHN 4:23

Resurrection

A rising again; chiefly, the revival of the dead of the human race, or their return from the grave

---

It is important that we learn to live on the resurrection side of the cross. Jesus was crucified and raised from the dead so that we might no longer be stuck in sin, living lowly, wretched, miserable lives.

Many people wear a necklace called a crucifix, which is an emblem of Jesus hanging on the cross. Often we see a crucifix in a church with Jesus hanging on it. I know it is done to remember and honor Him, and I am not against it, but the truth is that He is not on the cross any longer.

Jesus is seated in heavenly places with His Father, and He has also lifted us above the low level of thinking and living of most of the world. We can learn to live on the resurrection side of the cross—that's where the power is!

And with great strength and ability and power the apostles delivered their testimony to the resurrection of the Lord Jesus, and great grace (loving-kindness and favor and goodwill) rested richly upon them all.

ACTS 4:33

Big

Great in spirit; lofty; brave

I don't think it's dangerous to have a good opinion of yourself (in Christ), but I do think *it is dangerous not to*. The truth is you cannot rise above what you think. We are all limited by our own thinking.

If we think small, we will live small. And if we think big, we will live big. It's all about our view of God and our faith in what He wants to do in and through our lives.

God wants us to realize how big He is, and He wants us to be bold enough to think big thoughts. God did not chastise David because he thought he could kill

Goliath—He was proud of him! David knew that his victory was in God and not in himself, but he was confident and courageous and refused to live small.

> *Then said David to the Philistine, You come to me with a sword, a spear, and a javelin, but I come to you in the name of the Lord of hosts, the God of the ranks of Israel, Whom you have defied.*   1 SAMUEL 17:45

Control

**To exercise authoritative or
dominating influence over; direct**

When we worry about a situation or a
trouble, we are searching for answers to
our problems, hoping we will find a way
to control circumstances in our lives. But
the truth is that we were never in control
anyway, because God is.

Instead of using our power to attempt
to control situations and people, we can
use it to control ourselves. Instead of worrying about things we cannot control, we
can control our worry!

We will never lower our stress levels unless we learn to think properly. By

"properly," I mean believing the best while trusting God to take care of our problems. We may not be in control of the situation around us, but God is. All we have to do is trust Him and allow Him to do His good work in our lives.

And in [exercising] knowledge [develop] self-control, and in [exercising] self-control [develop] steadfastness (patience, endurance).   2 PETER 1:6

Decision

Determination, as of a question or doubt; final judgment or opinion

---

God doesn't always give us exact and specific directions, but He does guide us as we go through life trusting Him. He expects us to follow His Word, His Spirit, and His wisdom.

Keep your life simple by not doing anything you don't have peace about or that is not wise. Trust God to guide you daily, and boldly follow Him.

Don't be afraid to make decisions. Pray, and then follow what God puts in your heart. If you do make a mistake, you can trust Him to guide you back onto the right path.

In all your ways know, recognize, and acknowledge Him, and He will direct and make straight and plain your paths.

PROVERBS 3:6

Laugh

Convulsive merriment

Laughter is wonderful! When we laugh, we momentarily forget all of our concerns and struggles. It energizes us and is one of the healthiest things we can do.

I heard that the average child laughs 150 times a day, while the average adult only laughs four to eight times a day. It is no wonder that God tells us in His word that we must become like little children (see Matthew 18:3).

We often worry too much, trying to figure too many things out, and we become so intense that we forget to laugh at ourselves, as well as many other things in life.

Laughter can pull a person out of depression and despair, and it can turn an ordinary day into a memorable one. I strongly encourage you to find some people who make you laugh and spend more time with them. Laughter is possibly more important than you know.

Then were our mouths filled with laughter, and our tongues with singing.   PSALM 126:2

Normal

Conforming with, adhering to, or constituting a standard, pattern, level, or type

---

Living by faith in God takes the pressure off of us and allows us to enjoy all of life in a greater way. Faith is God's will, and I believe it can and should become our normal way of life.

The Bible says in Hebrews 11:6 that without faith we cannot please God. Romans 14:23 says that anything we do that is not done in faith is sin. Romans 1:17 says that righteousness is revealed in God's Word, and that it leads us from faith to faith.

To me this means that we can be in faith at all times. It can be our new normal!

Faith is trusting in what God says in His Word, even though you may not have any evidence of its reality yet. Faith is what connects us to God, it is how we receive from Him, and it can be our normal way to live.

And Jesus, replying, said to them, Have faith in God [constantly].   MARK 11:22

Freedom

A state of exemption from the power or control of another; liberty; exemption from slavery, servitude, or confinement

---

Jesus died so we could be free from the slavery of sin and overcome the attacks of the enemy, who "comes only in order to steal and kill and destroy" (John 10:10). The devil will often try to steal or destroy our faith in God through fear.

It is important to realize that our fears not only affect us, but they can also affect the people around us. Nothing is more uncomfortable to me than having to tip-toe around a person because they have fears that make them touchy, nervous, and uptight. I feel sorry for them, and I pray for them but, ultimately, fear cannot be conquered unless we recognize it and confront it.

You may be the way I was—afraid other people will not approve of you or afraid of an authority figure in your life. Whether you struggle with this fear or other fears, the path to freedom is the same: Study God's Word and apply it to your life; pray and ask God to help you face the fear and conquer it.

In [this] freedom Christ has made us free
[and completely liberated us]; stand fast then,
and do not be hampered and held ensnared
and submit again to a yoke of slavery [which
you have once put off].   GALATIANS 5:1

Abundant

Plentiful; in great quantity; fully sufficient

I believe we should develop what I call an abundant mind-set—one that believes God will always provide whatever we need in every situation.

This is God's promise throughout Scripture, and part of His nature is to provide for His children. In fact, in the Old Testament, one of the Hebrew names of God is "Jehovah-Jireh," which means, "The Lord Our Provider."

You and I are God's children. He is our Father, and He delights in providing for us just as natural parents delight in helping their children. Clearly, all the resources of heaven and earth are at His disposal, so there is nothing we need that He cannot provide. He loves us and it is His delight to hear our requests and abundantly provide.

Though He was [so very] rich, yet for your sakes He became [so very] poor, in order that by His poverty you might become enriched (abundantly supplied).

2 CORINTHIANS 8:9

Look

To direct the eye toward an object, with the intention of seeing it

---

If we look around at our circumstances excessively, we may end up terrified and dismayed, which means that we feel there is no way out of our problems or no way to reach our goals. With God there is always a way, because He is the Way.

God's Word tells us to look up, for redemption is drawing close (see Luke 21:28). If we look up with an expectant attitude it prevents us from being downcast.

God told Lot and his wife not to look back at Sodom and Gomorrah (see Genesis

19:17). The apostle Paul states that the one thing most important to him was to look away from what was behind to what was ahead (see Philippians 3:13).

Looking at the right thing is very important. Keep your eyes on Jesus and expect good things daily—that will keep you encouraged at all times.

They looked to Him and were radiant;
their faces shall never blush for shame or be
confused.   PSALM 34:5

Finisher

One who completely performs through to the end

_____

It is easy to begin a new thing. When something is new, it is exciting, and at the beginning, we have no idea how long it will take or how difficult it might be to see it all the way through to the finish.

I don't get overly excited anymore just because people tell me about a new thing they are beginning. I encourage them, but I don't assume that they will finish just because they have begun. Lots of people have a great idea but quit somewhere along the way when things become difficult.

But it doesn't have to be this way. If you

have the courage to press on when things are hard, God will help you to finish what you've started. I believe you can be a finisher, but it does require determination. I want to encourage you to set your mind and keep it set on finishing your race and obtaining the prize.

Let us run with patient endurance and steady and active persistence the appointed course of the race that is set before us.

HEBREWS 12:1

Expect

To look forward to the probable occurrence or appearance of

Godly expectation and anxiety are the exact opposites. A sense of expectation assumes God is going to do something good; anxiety assumes that the worst is going to happen.

I encourage you to expect God's goodness instead of being anxious that things won't work out. When we live with positive anticipation, it produces joy and opens the door for God's best in our lives.

God is good, and He wants us to expect Him to be good to us (see Isaiah 30:18). God is waiting to help us with everything we need to do in life. All He wants is to be invited to help us. Put your hope and expectation in God's promises and be excited to see what He will do in your life today and every day.

[For it is He] Who rescued and saved us from such a perilous death, and He will still rescue and save us; in and on Him we have set our hope (our joyful and confident expectation) that He will again deliver us.

2 CORINTHIANS 1:10

Risk-Taker

An individual who willfully exposes himself or herself to activities that others regard as hazardous

---

Most of us know someone in life whom we admire. We are in awe of this person's accomplishments, and we wish we could have been the ones who did what he or she did. A healthy admiration of someone can be a good motivator as long as we're not comparing ourselves to another person.

The thing we may not realize is that the person took risks to get where he or she is. Accomplishments are never met without bold action steps. I recently heard someone say, "If you're not failing occasionally, then you're not taking risks." This is so true!

It is virtually impossible to do great things without taking risks. We should do what we do based on biblical principles of wisdom, but it is not God's will for us to do absolutely nothing. Wayne Gretzky said it this way: "You'll always miss 100 percent of the shots you never take."

I am the Good Shepherd. The Good Shepherd risks and lays down His [own] life for the sheep.   JOHN 10:11

Solitude

**The state or quality of being alone
or remote from others**

One of the things we need more of in our society is solitude. We live in a noisy, high-pressure, busy world, where more is expected of most of us than we can possibly do. The world more than likely won't change, but we can. One of the main things that combats and offsets stress is solitude or quiet.

I absolutely love quiet times! I have discovered that even five minutes of quiet and solitude can restore my soul to a restful place and relieve stress. It gives me time to actually breathe deeply and do nothing.

If you're not used to quiet times, you may have to build up an ability to be quiet. If it is difficult for you, then start with a few minutes three or four times a day, and gradually increase your comfort level. Solitude offers a great chance to rest and refresh your soul and spirit. You'll be glad you learned to value this time.

And after He had dismissed the multitudes, He went up into the hills by Himself to pray. When it was evening, He was still there alone.   MATTHEW 14:23

Energize

To give strength or force to; to give active vigor to

All of our thoughts, good or bad, have an effect on our physical being. The mind and body are definitely connected. Positive, hopeful thoughts energize our soul and physical bodies, whereas negative, hopeless thoughts drain our energy.

Physical tiredness is not always a result of wrong thinking. We can certainly have a sickness or disease that leads to a loss of energy, or we may even wake up tired for no known reason. But we do know that science and medical technology verify that the mind and body have a close connection, and that our thinking does have a direct effect on our body.

Our bodies are like automobiles that God provides for us to drive around on earth. If we want them to perform to their maximum ability and be energized, then we need to choose to think in ways that will help fuel them.

It is the same God Who inspires and energizes them all in all.   1 CORINTHIANS 12:6

Forgiving

**Inclined to overlook offenses;
mild; merciful; compassionate**

We all get hurt at times, and it can be difficult to forgive others because we don't want them to get away with anything. But when you forgive, you allow God to deal with the person who hurt you. You remove yourself from the position of judge (a position that wasn't meant for you anyway), and you let God handle the offense that was perpetrated against you.

You'll be amazed at how much better you'll feel—physically, emotionally, and spiritually—when you choose to let go of the bitterness of unforgiveness. Don't think about how unfair it is; just do it because God has asked you to, and because you trust Him and His ways.

Notice I said, "when you choose to let go" of bitterness. Forgiveness is a choice. It doesn't happen accidentally. You can decide that you are going to be a forgiving person because God gives you the grace to do it.

And become useful and helpful and kind to one another, tenderhearted (compassionate, understanding, loving-hearted), forgiving one another [readily and freely], as God in Christ forgave you.   EPHESIANS 4:32

Begin

To do the first act; to enter upon something new; to take the first step

---

We may not know exactly where we're going or exactly how long it will take us to get there, but we still need to begin moving in the direction God is calling us.

- You may not know how your finances are going to work out, but you feel God is telling you to give a financial gift to a hurting family.
- You may not know for sure if you'll ever be in full-time ministry, but you feel God calling

you to begin a Bible study at your church.

- You may not know how you could ever change your diet completely, but you can begin by resisting those sweets tonight.

- You may not know how you can ever fully forgive the person who hurt you, but you feel God calling you to begin praying for that person today.

That's how faith begins. You begin moving in the direction of God's will one decision at a time.

Who dares despise the day of small things...?

ZECHARIAH 4:10 (NIV)

Possible

**That may be or exist; that may
be now, or may happen or come
to pass; that may be done; not
contrary to the nature of things**

If there are no impossibilities then we can
live in constant victory and nothing can
threaten us or make us feel afraid of the
future.

With men a great deal is impossible,
but with God all things are possible (see
Mark 10:27). Everything that is in the will
of God will be accomplished in His way
and timing. There is nothing too big, too
hard, or too overwhelming for God.

Is life too much for us? Is there anything

that we just cannot handle? Not according to God, for He says through the apostle Paul that we can do all things through Christ Who is our Strength. We are ready for anything and equal to anything through Him Who infused inner strength into us (see Philippians 4:13).

Live your life boldly, knowing that God will help you.

Jesus glanced around at them and said, With men [it is] impossible, but not with God; for all things are possible with God.

MARK 10:27

Creator

The thing that creates, produces, or causes

Just how sufficient are we without God? We had nothing to do with being born, no control over our nationality or the color of our skin, and we did not control our ancestry or the basic mental and physical abilities we were born with.

A power no one understands keeps our heart beating, our lungs taking in air, our blood circulating, and our body temperature up.

A simple study of the human body surely must tell us that we have a Divine Creator. What a tragedy to believe we evolved from apes. A surgeon can cut through human tissue, but, by a miracle no one understands, the body heals itself. You are a miracle created by God, and I encourage you to believe that with all your heart.

> *For it was in Him that all things were created, in heaven and on earth, things seen and things unseen, whether thrones, dominions, rulers, or authorities; all things were created and exist through Him [by His service, intervention] and in and for Him.*
>
> COLOSSIANS 1:16

Image

A copy, representation, or likeness

How you see yourself is your image of you. It is like a picture you carry in your mental wallet and it affects all of your words, emotions, actions, and decisions.

If you see yourself as someone who cannot control him- or herself, then that is the way you will be. But, if you see yourself as a person who has discipline and self-control (see 2 Timothy 1:7), then you will manifest discipline and self-control. If God says that we have a spirit of discipline and self-control then we need to think and say that we have a spirit of discipline and self-control. If you will see yourself the way He sees you, then you will become what He says you are.

We must remember that God sees the end from the beginning. He sees you as you can be and if you will agree with Him, you will see it come to pass.

And all of us, as with unveiled face, [because we] continued to behold [in the Word of God] as in a mirror the glory of the Lord, are constantly being transfigured into His very own image.   2 CORINTHIANS 3:18

Aware

Conscious; cautious

Habits are behaviors that we often do unconsciously, and to break bad ones we have to become conscious and aware that we are doing them, and choose to replace them with good habits.

Breaking bad habits is a process, and if you are a person who gives up easily, you won't get very far. So make a decision that you are in it for the long haul and that you are willing to have the pain for the gain.

Anything worth having in life is going to take a concentrated effort. With God's help, a determined attitude, and an awareness that a bad habit needs to be broken, you can have victory—be encouraged that you can break that bad habit, with God's help, and replace it with a good one.

Therefore, my beloved brethren, be firm (steadfast), immovable, always abounding in the work of the Lord... knowing and being continually aware that your labor in the Lord is not futile [it is never wasted or to no purpose].   1 CORINTHIANS 15:58

Mystery

A profound secret; something wholly unknown or something kept cautiously concealed

---

We might say that life is a mystery unfolding. As teenagers and young adults we try to formulate a plan for the future, but in reality, it is a mystery what our lives will hold. Not knowing everything is what urges us to seek God!

God is actually very fond of mystery. We can start with the mystery of our birth. The Bible says we are formed in secret and in the region of mystery (our mother's womb) (see Psalm 139:15). Job said the dealings of God with the ungodly are a mystery (see Job 21:16). And in Mark 4:11, the kingdom of God is said to be a mystery.

You may have some sort of a plan for the future, and that is good, but only God knows for sure what will happen. Thankfully, you can live in peace, trusting God with whatever happens. Be assured that God will guide you, He will be with you, and, therefore, you have nothing to fear.

Call to Me and I will answer you and show you great and mighty things, fenced in and hidden, which you do not know (do not distinguish and recognize, have knowledge of and understand).   JEREMIAH 33:3

Shepherd

A man employed in tending, feeding, and guarding sheep in the pasture

---

David said that the Lord is our Shepherd and we shall not lack (see Psalm 23:1). A good shepherd takes care of his sheep, and Jesus is called the Good Shepherd (see John 10:11–14).

God told the Israelites that He would lead them into a land where they would eat food without shortage and lack nothing in it (see Deuteronomy 8:7–10). God's Word to us today is no different from what it was to them. We don't have to fear lack. God will provide whatever you need in any situation.

Our responsibility is to simply follow the leading of our Good Shepherd. He leads us to the best life we can possibly have. The way He takes us might be different than we had planned, but as we obediently follow Him, we will see it unfold and enjoy His goodness.

For you were going astray like [so many] sheep, but now you have come back to the Shepherd and Guardian (the Bishop) of your souls.   1 PETER 2:25

Obstacle

That which opposes; any thing that stands in the way and hinders progress; hindrance; obstruction

---

I've discovered that with God's guidance we can remove every obstacle that could possibly prevent us from finishing our race and obtaining our prize. At times He places obstacles in our path in order to test and strengthen our faith, but they are never meant to defeat us.

We are strengthened as we deal with difficulties. Even though it's not easy as we go through them, these dilemmas are benefiting us—they are preparing us for bigger things in the future. But if we run from every obstacle, we will never grow and become stronger in our faith and abilities.

When dealing with obstacles today or in the future, don't shrink back. Instead, boldly go forward, remembering that with God's help, the obstacles will be removed.

A voice of one who cries: Prepare in the wilderness the way of the Lord [clear away the obstacles]; make straight and smooth in the desert a highway for our God! ISAIAH 40:3

Partner

One that is united or associated with another or others in an activity or a sphere of common interest

---

It is comforting to know that with God as our partner, we can do whatever we need to do in life, no matter how challenging it is. Be aware that God is with you at all times and lean on Him.

Because of our tendency to be self-reliant, we often fail to lean on God. Instead, we think we have to do it all and we quickly become weary and give up.

We are partners with God. We cannot do His part and He will not do our part.

When we pray, we should not expect God to do everything for us; we should listen for His direction and do what He asks us to do, knowing that He will never fail to do the part that only He can do. And He will always strengthen us and give us the ability to do what we must do.

I have strength for all things in Christ Who empowers me [I am ready for anything and equal to anything through Him Who infuses inner strength into me; I am self-sufficient in Christ's sufficiency].   PHILIPPIANS 4:13

Other

A different person or thing

Many of our trials in life are the result of other people. Someone else's failure, carelessness, ignorance, or sin affects us, and we understandably pray for God to change him or her.

Even though we want others to change and treat us better, I have discovered that it is better for me to focus on how I treat people than on how they treat me. Sometimes God uses the things about people that irritate us to change us. He makes us more tolerant and patient and enables us to love unconditionally.

Pray for people, but don't forget to pray

for yourself that your reaction to their
weaknesses will be what God wants it
to be.

Blessed (happy, fortunate, to be envied) are
those who observe justice [treating others
fairly] and who do right and are in right
standing with God at all times.

                                    PSALM 106:3

Gifts

Power; faculty; some quality or endowment conferred by the author of our nature

---

God has given you the gifts, talents, abilities, and grace you need to do His will in life. God's grace is actually His power, and He will not only give you grace but promises grace and more grace (see James 4:6). God gifted you for a reason; He has a powerful plan for your life. Whatever He has planned for you to do, He will empower you to do it.

God never runs out of power—and His power is available to you!

If you don't keep the right mind-set,

the enemy can defeat you with thoughts of inadequacy, but if you make up your mind that you are gifted by God and that you can do what you need to do, you'll enjoy victory—not in your own strength, but with the strength, gifts, and grace God gives you.

Having gifts (faculties, talents, qualities) that differ according to the grace given us, let us use them.　ROMANS 12:6

Experience

Knowledge derived from trials, use, practice, or from a series of observations

---

Consider your life. Are there situations you now handle well that would have previously made you feel fearful and anxious? Of course there are. As you have been walking with God, He has been strengthening you through experience and hardening you to difficulties.

In the same way, I can also assure you and encourage you that some of the things bothering you right now will not affect you the same way in the future. We often struggle when we do certain things for the first time. But after gaining some experience, that struggle is no longer present. We must press through the feelings, gain some experience leaning on God, and never allow circumstances to control us.

> *And they shall know [from personal*
> *experience] that I am the Lord their God,*
> *Who brought them forth out of the land of*
> *Egypt that I might dwell among them; I am*
> *the Lord their God.*   EXODUS 29:46

Race

**A progress; a course; a movement
or progression of any kind**

The apostle Paul referred to life as a race. I think most of us want to run our race well and be everything God intends for us to be...and to enjoy it along the way.

Great joy comes with finishing the race God has called you to run. Enjoy the journey and keep your eyes on the prize. Jesus endured the cross for the joy of obtaining the prize before Him (see Hebrews 12:2).

As Paul neared the end of his journey on earth, he wrote that he had "finished the race" (see 2 Timothy 4:7). In this verse, he was basically saying: *I have been through a lot. But I am still here. The enemy tried to get me to quit my race, but he did not succeed!*

At the end of your life, you want to be able to say the same thing. Don't get discouraged. Don't quit. Run your race well!

I have fought the good (worthy, honorable, and noble) fight, I have finished the race, I have kept (firmly held) the faith.

2 TIMOTHY 4:7

Rested

To cease motion, work, or activity, especially in order to become refreshed

In Matthew 11:28–29, Jesus speaks of rest two times. One reference is to the rest of salvation, and the other is the rest we need for daily life.

The invitation to come to Him and find rest (v. 28) is in reference to receiving salvation through faith in Jesus Christ. When we do that, we find an immediate type of rest that we have not experienced previously. We enjoy knowing that our sins are forgiven and that we are loved and accepted by God.

We have the rest of no longer being afraid of death, because we know that when we die, we will simply pass from this earthly realm into the heavenly realm where we will live forever in God's Presence.

We also have the privilege of entering God's rest about anything that overwhelms or concerns us. We can cast our care on Him because He cares for us.

Come to Me, all you who labor and are heavy-laden and overburdened, and I will cause you to rest. [I will ease and relieve and refresh your souls.] MATTHEW 11:28

Refreshed

Cooled; invigorated; revived; cheered

The rest of salvation is wonderful, but we also need rest in our daily lives, and Jesus tells us how to have that when He says, "Take My yoke upon you ... and you will find rest (relief and ease and refreshment ...)" (Matthew 11:29).

A yoke is a device used to couple two animals together, such as the pairing of oxen used to pull a plow for farming. If we stay "yoked" (very close) to Jesus, He will refresh us by balancing out our load in life, and we will learn how He responds to every situation.

To live a refreshed life, it is important that we walk in step with Jesus. When feelings of frustration, fear, or discouragement come along, we can give those to Him and allow Him to carry the load. You don't have to carry any burden alone; you can always give it to God in order to keep going.

Take My yoke upon you and learn of Me, for I am gentle (meek) and humble (lowly) in heart, and you will find rest (relief and ease and refreshment and recreation and blessed quiet) for your souls.   MATTHEW 11:29

Overcoming

To conquer; to vanquish; to subdue

There are many things in the world that can make us angry, but we can defeat the emotion of anger by continuing to do good at all times.

Paul told the Corinthians they should forgive in order to keep Satan from getting an advantage over them (see 2 Corinthians 2:10–11). He told the Ephesians if they stayed angry, it would open a door for the devil and give him opportunity (see Ephesians 4:27).

One of the best ways to defeat evil is by finding people you can be good to. The world is full of needs, and as we stay busy meeting those needs, we can be assured that God will always take care of us.

I encourage you to walk in wisdom. Don't let evil people or the negative emotion of anger control your life. Make a decision right now to overcome anger with God's help. I believe it will open a door for God's blessings to flow into your life in a new way.

Do not let yourself be overcome by evil, but
overcome (master) evil with good.

ROMANS 12:21

Forget

**To lose the remembrance of; to let
go from the memory**

We all make mistakes in life, and sometimes we hold on to them and it keeps us
from moving forward and making progress in our walk with God. If you can make
restitution for something you did in the
past and make it better, by all means you
should do that. However, if there is nothing you can do about a mistake or short-
coming from your past, the best thing you
can do is let it go. It's not going to do you
any good to bury yourself in regret.

Regret is not faith. Regret looks at the
mistake without looking at God's ability

to take care of it. Our mistakes are not greater than God's mercy. Our badness is not greater than God's goodness.

Hebrews 8:12 says: "For I will be merciful and gracious toward their sins and I will remember their deeds of unrighteousness no more." Since God chooses to forgive and forget your sins, you can choose to forgive yourself and forget your sins, too.

One thing I do [it is my one aspiration]: forgetting what lies behind and straining forward to what lies ahead, I press on toward the goal.   PHILIPPIANS 3:13–14

Recess

A temporary cessation of the customary activities of an engagement, occupation, or pursuit

——————————

As a new creation in Christ (see 2 Corinthians 5:17), God's plan is for you to be a disciplined person, living with goals, and taking steps toward success. It is also important that you plan to do things you enjoy. Take time for recess!

Make that latte and enjoy drinking it. Take that walk in the park. Plan that family vacation. Enjoy that lunch hour. Go out with friends. Save up and buy that pair of shoes.

I have found that I don't discipline myself without a plan, and I have also found that I am more likely to do things I enjoy if I plan them, too.

God has given us a spirit of discipline and self-control, and we all need to exercise those, but He has also given us a need for rest and relaxation. Don't be afraid to take a break every once in a while. Recess is important—so enjoy it.

And He said to them, [As for you] come away by yourselves to a deserted place, and rest a while.   MARK 6:31

Thoughtful

**Attentive; careful; having the
mind directed to an object**

Since our thoughts do affect the way we
relate to people and the world around us, it
is helpful to learn to be thoughtful.

Take time to think through your day
before you begin it. Of course, we don't
know everything a day will hold, but we all,
hopefully, have some plan. Being thoughtful about your day on purpose is very
different from worrying about it. Being
thoughtful about the parts of your day that
you know about helps you behave the way
that pleases God instead of just reacting to
things out of a thoughtless habit.

Things will happen today that you are not planning, but you can even plan to respond calmly to things that are unexpected. Whatever you do, plan to enjoy it! Today is a gift from God, and I urge you not to waste it.

[Thoughtfully and attentively] consider Jesus, the Apostle and High Priest Whom we confessed [as ours when we embraced the Christian faith].   HEBREWS 3:1

Lean

To bend or incline so as to rest on something

Trusting God is much better than trying to find a reason for everything that happens that you don't like or understand. God does give us understanding in many things, but He also may choose to ask us to trust Him without understanding.

The very nature of trust requires that we have some unanswered questions in life. To lean on God means to put the weight of your burden on Him, rather than trying to carry it by yourself.

God is waiting with open arms to carry your load if you are ready to release it to

Him. You may not know how to solve your problem, but you can lean on the One Who does know.

Lean on, trust in, and be confident in the
Lord with all your heart and mind and do not
rely on your own insight or understanding.

PROVERBS 3:5

Solution

A method or process of dealing with a problem

Stress is an ever-present danger, but there are many simple and effective ways to resist it. Let me share a few solutions with you:

- Change your schedule, and leave margin in it so you're not always rushing.
- Take time to do things you enjoy instead of focusing excessively on work.
- Have a plan, but don't get upset if your plan is interrupted for valid reasons.

- Make better choices about what you eat, because the kind of fuel you put in your body determines how well it functions.
- Have a regular bedtime, and get good sleep.
- Don't try to make everybody happy all the time at the cost of living with unhealthy stress.
- Say no when you need to.

With God's help you can solve the stress problem.

Do not let your heart be troubled, nor let it be afraid. [Let My perfect peace calm you in every circumstance and give you courage and strength for every challenge.]

JOHN 14:27 (AMP)

Fullest

Containing all that is normal or possible

Whether we are ready or not, someday our lives will come to an end. We don't get a second chance here on this earth, so it is crucial that we live the lives we have to the fullest.

Your life is a precious gift from God, and it would be tragic if you lived it unhappily. That is why you should make it a daily habit to choose to be happy. Put the happy habit on your list of good habits to make, and as you develop it, the sad or mad habits will find no place in your life.

Having a life worth living doesn't just

happen by accident; it is something we can choose on purpose. I can truly say that I've become a genuinely happy person, but I wasn't that way until I made the choice to be happy. Don't wait for a circumstance or a person to make you happy; be happy on purpose.

I came that they may have and enjoy life, and have it in abundance (to the full, till it overflows).   JOHN 10:10

Need

necessity; requirement

_____

Many times we think of needs in terms of the basic necessities of life—food, shelter, clothing, and finances to purchase these things.

These represent our physical needs, but I believe God created us to need more than these essentials. Our needs are varied. We don't simply need money, nourishment, a roof over our heads and clothes to wear. We also need wisdom, strength, health, friends and loved ones; and we need the gifts and talents and abilities to help us do what we are supposed to do in life.

We need many things, and God is

willing to meet all our needs as we obey and trust Him. We can believe that He wants to provide for us. We can develop an expectant mind-set in this area.

And my God will liberally supply (fill to the full) your every need according to His riches in glory in Christ Jesus. PHILIPPIANS 4:19

Follow

To go after or behind; to walk, ride, or move behind, but in the same direction

---

God has sent the Holy Spirit to live in our hearts, to lead, guide, and direct us into all truth and the best life that we can have. But He cannot lead us anywhere if we are not willing to follow.

The apostle Paul had an amazing life and ministry, and we can see in his writing that he followed the leadership of the Holy Spirit to the best of his ability. Yet there were times when he made mistakes. Yes, I said that Paul made mistakes. There were times when God had to re-route Paul to a different city or ministry opportunity.

Paul did not let the fear of being wrong keep him from continually learning how to follow the Holy Spirit's direction. If your heart is right and you do make a mistake, God will lovingly help you see it and guide you into the right thing.

> *Therefore be imitators of God [copy Him and follow His example], as well-beloved children [imitate their father].*   EPHESIANS 5:1

Being

Existence

_____

We tend to think that our existence is only justified when we are *doing* something, but that is not true. We are human *beings*, not human *doings*.

God doesn't love us more when we are doing something than He does when we are enjoying quiet. Our busyness makes us feel important, but it doesn't make us more important to God.

Many people feel more acceptable when they are working than at any other time. Some of that comes from the way they were raised; some of it is just their personality or work ethic. Whatever the reason is, the result is the same. Too much activity without any rest can damage your future and prevent you from enjoying the present.

Let's thank God and live in the reality that He has not created us to merely do, but also to be.

For in Him we live and move and have our being.   ACTS 17:28

You

The one or ones being addressed

God thinks that you are special and He celebrates you all the time. He is ready and willing to help you anytime you need Him to.

What is your attitude toward you? Are you worth a celebration? In the Bible we are told to sing, shout, rejoice, and be in high spirits because God has taken away the judgment that was against us. He has come to live in the midst of us, and we have no need to fear. Because He loves us, He does not even mention past sins, and He exults over us with singing (see Zephaniah 3:14–17).

These Scriptures don't say God is sitting in heaven mourning because you make mistakes and are not all that He hoped you would be. They say that you should be in high spirits because God loves you and is singing over you. What a great way to view yourself.

The Lord your God is in your midst, a warrior who saves. He will rejoice over you with joy; He will be quiet in His love [making no mention of your past sins], He will rejoice over you with shouts of joy.

ZEPHANIAH 3:17 AMP

Aspiration

The act of ardently desiring what is noble or spiritual

Paul learned the power of overcoming his past. In Philippians 3:13 he said it was his aim—his "one aspiration"—to forget what was behind him, and God used him mightily.

I wonder what would happen in your life if you made it your one aspiration to move past your past. Just imagine what God could do in your life if you stopped focusing on the events of yesterday. I believe He would totally revolutionize every area of your life.

To move forward into God's best is

going to take determination. There are lots of things that want to hold you back, including events from your past. But if you'll make it your one aspiration, you can move past yesterday, enjoy today, and go boldly into tomorrow.

Do not [earnestly] remember the former things; neither consider the things of old. Behold, I am doing a new thing! Now it springs forth; do you not perceive and know it and will you not give heed to it?   ISAIAH 43:18–19

Stop

To put an end to any motion or action

I share in my teaching that we often study the steps of Jesus but fail to study the stops of Jesus. We all need to learn when to stop.

Jesus stopped what He was doing to listen to people and to help them. He stopped to rest, to have dinner with friends, to go to a wedding, and to do lots of other simple but important things.

When Jesus visited Mary and Martha, Mary knew when to stop, but Martha didn't. Mary sat at Jesus' feet so she would not miss the moment, but Martha just kept working (see Luke 10:38–41).

I wonder how many times in life we miss the moment because we don't know when to stop.

Let be and be still, and know (recognize and understand) that I am God. I will be exalted among the nations! I will be exalted in the earth!   PSALM 46:10

Coach

A person who gives instruction, as in singing or acting

Life coaches have become very popular today. They are people who help clients learn how to live their lives in the best way possible, and their training covers many areas of life.

You may have even wished that you could have a coach for all areas of life to remind you when you are doing the wrong thing so that you can begin doing the right thing. If that is true, then I have good news for you. You can count on your life coach, the Holy Spirit, to always teach you and lead you out of harmful behaviors and into good ones. He brings us into truth and guides and directs us.

Life coaches are helpful to a lot of people, and if you want to pay one you can, but you already have the best one that has ever been available: the Holy Spirit.

And when He comes, He will convict and convince the world and bring demonstration to it about sin and about righteousness.

JOHN 16:8

Enable

To supply with power, physical or moral; to furnish with sufficient power or ability

---

I hear so many people make comments such as, "This is too hard. I just can't do this. It's too much for me." But I need to tell you, as a believer in Jesus Christ, you are full of the Spirit of God, and nothing is too difficult for you if God is leading you to do it.

God will not call you to do anything He will not enable and empower you to do. He will not allow you to go through anything that is impossible for you.

Although God never authors bad things,

He does use them to help us grow stronger in our faith. For example, He may use a grouchy person to help us become more patient. God did not cause the person to be grouchy, but neither does He remove them from our lives when we ask Him to. Instead, He uses them to enable us to change and become more like Christ.

But He said to me, My grace (My favor and loving-kindness and mercy) is enough for you [sufficient against any danger and enables you to bear the trouble...

2 CORINTHIANS 12:9

Weapon

An instrument for contest or for combating enemies

Every time we suffer emotional pain, injustices, or offenses, we need to remember that people are not our enemies; Satan is our enemy. God has given us a secret weapon, one that is sure to defeat the devil and destroy his strategies and plans.

This weapon is truly important and powerful. It's found in Romans 12:21: "Do not let yourself be overcome by evil, but overcome (master) evil with good."

You have a secret weapon against the enemy, and he absolutely hates it because he knows he cannot stand against it. I call it a secret weapon because most people miss it. Your weapon is your God-given ability to be good to people who offend you. Your flesh may want revenge, but God says press through your pain by repaying evil with good.

> *For the weapons of our warfare are not*
> *physical [weapons of flesh and blood], but*
> *they are mighty before God for the overthrow*
> *and destruction of strongholds.*
>
> 2 CORINTHIANS 10:4

Paid

The past tense of *pay*; provided due compensation

The enemy loves to remind you of your past. He takes the mistakes, disappointments, hurts, and offenses from former seasons in your life and replays them in your mind like broken records.

In between every verse of those same old condemning songs, he sings this chorus: "Now you have to pay. You have to pay for everything you did wrong. You have to pay! You have to pay!"

But I want to encourage you to reject the lies of the enemy. Just because you had a bad past doesn't mean you can't have a great future (see Jeremiah 29:11).

God's Word reminds you that Jesus has already paid the price for your sins, mistakes, and failures. There is nothing left for you to pay—Jesus paid it all.

You were bought with a price [purchased with a preciousness and paid for, made His own]. So then, honor God and bring glory to Him in your body.   1 CORINTHIANS 6:20

Train

To exercise; to discipline; to teach and form by practice

The writer of Ecclesiastes said we are to give our mind to what we are doing (see Ecclesiastes 5:1). I don't know about you, but I often find that difficult. My mind has a tendency to wander, and I have to keep calling it back to what is at hand.

The more we allow our minds to run wild, the wilder they will become, but they can be trained to focus, with some diligent effort.

You will never train and control your thoughts if you don't believe that you can. At any moment you can stop thinking about something you don't want to think about and start thinking about something you *do* want to think about.

Don't let your mind run your life, but instead choose your own thoughts carefully because they become your actions.

Train yourself toward godliness (piety),
[keeping yourself spiritually fit].

1 TIMOTHY 4:7

Reprioritize

To arrange or do in order of importance and urgency

Keeping our priorities in proper order is very important, and I have found that in order to do so, I have to make changes and adjustments fairly frequently.

Life seems to get too full sometimes without my even knowing how it got that way. We say yes to one thing and then another, we do a friend a favor, we feel we should attend an event because we don't want anybody to be offended, and on and on it goes.

When that happens, it is time to reprioritize. We make our schedules, and we are the only ones who can change them. The author of Hebrews said to look away from all that would distract us from Jesus, who is the Leader and Source of our faith (see Hebrews 12:2).

Always keep Jesus in the center of all that you do, and refuse to let anything distract you from Him.

This is He of Whom I said, After me comes a Man Who has priority over me [Who takes rank above me] because He was before me and existed before I did.   JOHN 1:30

Aggressively

Assertively, boldly, and energetically

Lying on the couch or leaning back in the recliner asking God to take care of everything that needs to be done is easy, but it leaves us idle and unfruitful and open to the attack of evil.

If our minds are empty of good thoughts, the devil can easily fill them with bad ones. If we are lazy and inactive, he can easily tempt us to do wrong and even sinful things.

The Bible tells us quite frequently to be active for it will keep us from being lazy and unfruitful. If we aggressively think about what we can do for others there will be no room in our minds for wrong thoughts.

We should aggressively seek to stay active—not overly involved lest we burn out—but involved enough to keep us going in the right direction.

But be doers of the Word [obey the message], and not merely listeners to it, betraying yourselves [into deception by reasoning contrary to the Truth].   JAMES 1:22

Foundation

The basis or groundwork; that on which anything stands, and by which it is supported

---

People have asked me through the years, "What has been the most difficult aspect or experience of your ministry?" I always respond, "Not giving up when we were laying the foundation."

Though we have faced our share of situations that tempted us to want to give up, nothing has been as challenging as staying diligent during those early years. We wanted a fruitful ministry, but we knew we needed a strong foundation before we could build one.

Whatever you believe God wants to do in your life, be patient as He brings it to pass. Don't long for too much too fast, but be thankful every day that God is establishing a foundation that will support the growth, expansion and new opportunities He will bring into your life at just the right time.

Through skillful and godly Wisdom is a house (a life, a home, a family) built, and by understanding it is established [on a sound and good foundation]. PROVERBS 24:3

Commitment

A pledge or promise

I discovered that the people in my life who didn't want to make a full commitment to serving God tried to keep me from doing so. People usually try to get us to do what they are doing, rather than giving us the freedom to make our own choices.

We must not give in to their pressure because eventually each of us will stand before God and give an account of our lives. We won't answer to people; we will answer to God, so we should be committed to Him and Him alone.

If you really want to develop a deeper relationship with God, you will have to take the chance that some friends or co-workers may not understand you. They may reject you or speak unkindly about you, but stay committed to God, keep pressing forward and don't let anything stop you.

> *For the eyes of the Lord range throughout the earth to strengthen those whose hearts are fully committed to him.*
>
> 2 CHRONICLES 16:9 (NIV)

Belief

In theology, faith, or a firm persuasion of the truths of religion

---

We need to come to the point in life where we decide whether we really believe what the Bible says or not. Is it our belief that Jesus took our sins upon Himself and that He took our punishment, rose from the dead, and is interceding for us before the Father right now? Is it our belief Jesus is our substitute and that what He did for us we do not have to do again? If we do believe He did these things for us, then we need to act on that belief and refuse to stay trapped in yesterday's mistakes. He always calls us to go forward and to forget what lies behind us.

We can't be of value to God while we're trapped in guilt and condemning feelings. Mature believers apply the work of the cross in their lives, accept by faith that Jesus shed His blood to forgive their sins, receive His forgiveness, and press on into the things God has called them to do without letting guilt hold them back.

So that your trust (belief, reliance, support, and confidence) may be in the Lord, I have made known these things to you today, even to you.   PROVERBS 22:19

Party

**A number of persons united in
opinion or design**

Jesus said that He came so we can have and
enjoy life (see John 10:10). When Jesus
invited people to become His disciples and
follow Him, He asked them if they wanted
to join His party. I realize He was talking
about His group, but I like to think that
traveling with Jesus was probably a lot of
fun as well as a lot of hard work.

Jesus told the rich, young ruler that we
read about in Luke 18 to lay aside his selfish lifestyle and join His party. The rich,
young ruler had money, but it controlled
him, and Jesus wanted him to learn that

real joy was not found in what we own but in living for the right purpose.

Repeatedly through the Gospels (Matthew, Mark, Luke, and John) we see Jesus inviting people to leave their lifestyles and side with His party, and He is still issuing that invitation today.

At once they left their nets and became His disciples [sided with His party and followed Him].   MATTHEW 4:20

Relief

The removal or alleviation of pain, grief, want, care, anxiety, toil, or distress

---

I spent a lot of years frustrated most of the time, and thankfully, I now know how to avoid frustration and find relief. Frustration is always caused by what the Bible calls works of the flesh, which are our human energy trying to do what only God can do.

Stop trying to change things or people you cannot change, and frustration disappears. We have two options in life and they are to either struggle or trust God. Since we cannot change people, we can change our attitude toward them.

You can find almost unbelievable relief by facing the fact that you cannot change another person. Sometimes what we want from people is unrealistic, and we have to learn to let them be who they are, but if they truly do need to change, God is the only One who can do it. Controlling ourselves should be our goal, not controlling someone else.

A new heart will I give you and a new spirit will I put within you, and I will take away the stony heart out of your flesh and give you a heart of flesh.   EZEKIEL 36:26

Pray

To ask with earnestness or zeal, as for a favor, or for something desirable; to entreat; to supplicate

---

You don't have to live life feeling as though you are going to explode any minute or thinking you simply cannot make it one more day.

If you're in a difficult marriage, the best thing you can do for yourself, before you do anything else, is spend time with God right away, every day. If your job entails great responsibility and high stress, the best thing you can do for yourself is to take some of your lunch break, and spend time with God. If you have a child who is challenging to raise and hard to deal with, spending time with God before you begin your day will be the best investment you can make.

Taking a few five-minute "spiritual vacations" throughout the day is also helpful. Pause for even a few minutes and pray or meditate on Scriptures that encourage and strengthen you.

But when you pray, go into your [most]
private room, and, closing the door, pray
to your Father, Who is in secret; and your
Father, Who sees in secret, will reward you in
the open.   MATTHEW 6:6

Hope

A desire of some good, accompanied with at least a slight expectation of obtaining it, or a belief that it is obtainable

---

Hope is the opposite of dread, and it is a close relative of faith. Hebrews 11:1 tells us faith is "the assurance (the confirmation, the title deed) of the things [we] hope for."

When we have hope, our outlook on life and the future is positive. We can have hope because we trust in God's love, His power to provide for us, and His ability to lead us in every situation. Hope keeps us from worrying, allows us to leave our unanswered questions in God's hands, empowers us to stay at peace, and enables us to believe the best about the days to come.

People with hope are happy, optimistic, and full of God's strength and courage.

O my God, I trust, lean on, rely on, and am confident in You. Let me not be put to shame or [my hope in You] be disappointed; let not my enemies triumph over me.   PSALM 25:2

Narrow

**Of little breadth; not wide or
broad; having little distance from
side to side**

If you want to reach any worthy goal at all
or do anything significant for God, you
will find you always have to go through a
narrow place.

Anytime God leads you toward a broader
place—a position of greater influence,
greater enjoyment in life, or a fulfilled
desire—you will have to squeeze through
a narrow place to get there. Your narrow place may be a time when you have
to walk away from negative relationships,
when you have to discipline your mouth

to speak positively instead of complaining, or choosing to work while others are entertaining themselves.

These kinds of disciplines will squeeze you and press you, but they will also lead you to the broad places and blessings God has for you.

But the gate is narrow (contracted by pressure) and the way is straitened and compressed that leads away to life, and few are those who find it.   MATTHEW 7:14

Heaven

The abode of God, the angels, and the souls of those who are granted salvation

---

Heaven, the eternal home of the believer in Jesus Christ, is described in the Bible as not only totally peaceful but also stunningly beautiful (see Revelation 21 and 22).

Having faith that this is our destiny delivers us from the fear of death. Death is not an unknown nothingness but a graduation into better things than what we have experienced on earth.

As Christians, we can truthfully say, "I will live in heaven forever!" Your address will change someday from earth to heaven, but you will never really die. What a joy to know that we have the hope of a beautiful, peaceful place where there will be no more tears, pain, or dying, and we will live in the actual Presence of God.

> *God will wipe away every tear from their eyes; and death shall be no more, neither shall there be anguish (sorrow and mourning) nor grief nor pain any more, for the old conditions and the former order of things have passed away.*   REVELATION 21:4

Abundantly

Fully; amply; plentifully; in a sufficient degree

Many people have a fear of not having enough—I know I did. My father was a very stingy man and never seemed to want me to have the basic things that other children and teenagers had. This left me with a deep-seated belief that I should expect only what I had to have in order to get by in life.

Later in life, through my relationship with God, I gradually learned to trust God for His abundance.

God wants to bless His children to have the best, not the least. He does exceedingly, abundantly, above and beyond all we dare to hope, ask, or think (see Ephesians 3:20). I encourage you to develop a mindset of abundance, not scarcity. Don't live in the fear of lack, for God promises that He will abundantly supply your every need.

Though He was [so very] rich, yet for your sakes He became [so very] poor, in order that by His poverty you might become enriched (abundantly supplied).

2 CORINTHIANS 8:9

Daily

Happening or being every day; done, bestowed, or enjoyed every day

---

We have the privilege of trusting God daily to meet every need that we have— faith to pay the bills, keep a good job, raise the kids, make marriage work, get along with people, and so on.

Daily faith is vital if we are going to eliminate stress and enjoy life. Faith leaves no room for worry and it drives out fear. Learning to trust God in every situation will help you overcome worry and anxiety.

Daily faith is filled with hopeful expectation and it never gives up. Each new day is a new opportunity to see God do something amazing. A saying I like is: "When faith goes to the market, it always takes a basket." Keep your basket handy because God may fill it at any moment.

Give us this day our daily bread.

MATTHEW 6:11

Generosity

The quality of giving abundantly; liberality in principle; a disposition to give liberally or to bestow favors

Greed steals the life of the greedy person, because he can never be satisfied. Greedy people cannot enjoy what they have because they are never genuinely content.

It is not wrong to want things. God has provided many beautiful things, and He wants His children to enjoy them. But He wants us to enjoy them with a proper attitude. That attitude should be one of gratitude, contentment, and a willingness to be generous to others.

We must fight against greed, and the

best way I know to do that is to develop the habit of generosity. Look for people to bless, friends and family and co-workers who have a need that you can meet. There are opportunities all around you to show generosity—you just need to look for them.

> *Thus you will be enriched in all things and in every way, so that you can be generous, and [your generosity as it is] administered by us will bring forth thanksgiving to God.*
>
> 2 CORINTHIANS 9:11

Passion

Zeal; ardor; vehement desire

———————

The new covenant of salvation through Jesus Christ is a new way of living. You may be in need of a new life. Perhaps you want a life that is truly filled with purpose, peace, joy, energy, passion, and enthusiasm. If that is the case, you can learn to recognize and follow the Holy Spirit, not people, not man-made rules, and not your own ideas. Jesus said, "Follow Me" (Matthew 4:19).

Only God's Spirit can energize your life and keep it from stagnating. If you learn to listen to Him, God will lead you in what to do to stay stirred up and enthusiastic about the life He has planned for you.

Living without enthusiasm and joy does not give glory to God. So if you're merely going through the motions, it's time to make a change. Give your whole heart passionately to God and His will for your life.

Whatever may be your task, work at it heartily (from the soul), as [something done] for the Lord and not for men.

COLOSSIANS 3:23

Altitude

Figuratively, high degree, superior excellence, or highest point of excellence

---

You have probably heard the saying, "Attitude determines altitude," and it really is true. A person with a good attitude and almost no physical advantages will go further in life than someone with a lot of advantages and a bad attitude.

No matter how qualified someone may be for a job, I refuse to work with negative people. They kill creativity and put a damper on enthusiasm and passion.

We flourish in a positive atmosphere, just as flowers flourish in proper amounts of sun and rain. One of the things I have learned during my journey with God is that there is nothing negative about Him. God is always positive, and if we want to go higher with Him, we will have to be the same way.

And set your minds and keep them set on
what is above (the higher things), not on the
things that are on the earth.

COLOSSIANS 3:2

Healing

To restore to health or soundness; cure

Some people believe God wants them to be sick. If that is the case, then I wonder why they go to the doctor and try to get well. I realize there are people who struggle with chronic illness, yet they are putting their faith in God because they believe He is the Healer. But regardless of whether we understand our circumstances, we need to know God's will; otherwise, we cannot release our faith and maintain our peace and joy while we're waiting to receive it.

In Matthew 5, 8, and 9, Jesus cleansed a leper and healed the centurion's servant,

Peter's mother-in-law, a paralyzed man, and a woman who had been bleeding for twelve years. He cast demons out of a man who was possessed and raised a girl from the dead. He opened the eyes of two blind men and gave a dumb man the ability to speak.

If we are going to believe the Word of God, we must believe God's nature is to heal and make whole. It is important to God that we have a prosperous life in all areas, including good health (see 3 John 2). If you are sick, keep trusting God for healing.

> *He personally bore our sins in His [own] body on the tree [as on an altar and offered Himself on it], that we might die (cease to exist) to sin and live to righteousness. By His wounds you have been healed.*   1 PETER 2:24

Dispense

To deal or divide out in parts or portions; to distribute

The love of God is in us because God puts His love in our hearts when we accept Jesus as our Savior, but it needs to be dispensed through us in order for it to help anyone else.

In Genesis 12:2, God told Abraham He would bless him and make him a person who dispensed blessings everywhere he went.

When I read that story, I am reminded of a bottle of hand lotion I have, one that has a pump on it. When I press the pump, it dispenses hand lotion. That's the way we can be with blessings. When people come near us, we can determine to dispense something good, something that will benefit them.

> *Let each of you esteem and look upon and be concerned for not [merely] his own interests, but also each for the interests of others.*
>
> PHILIPPIANS 2:4

Now

At the present time

I think it's important that we learn to enjoy "now moments"—the present moments in our lives.

Learning to be happy while you work is one way to do that, but there are many others. Begin now to think about what you can do to find more joy in every experience. The present moment in this life is all we're guaranteed, so don't wait until later—until you get married, until you retire, until you go on vacation, until your children finish college, until you have more money—to enjoy life.

Nobody knows what is going to happen

next in their lives or in the world. You are alive now, so make the most of the moments God gives you. Maximize them, embrace them, and celebrate them.

> *[It is that purpose and grace] which He now has made known and has fully disclosed and made real [to us] through the appearing of our Savior Christ Jesus.*   2 TIMOTHY 1:10

Obey

To submit to the direction or control of

_____

Whenever Christians are faced with God's Word, and it calls them to action but they refuse to obey, their own human reasoning is often the cause. They have deceived themselves into believing something other than the truth.

It is amazing how quickly we can talk ourselves out of doing something when deep down inside we really don't want to do it. James 1:22 is very clear when it says: "But be doers of the Word [obey the message], and not merely listeners to it, betraying yourselves [into deception by reasoning contrary to the Truth]."

When the Bible speaks about obeying the Lord, it is not a suggestion. God commands us to take action by being a doer of His Word, and when we are obedient, He promises we will be blessed.

Samuel said, Has the Lord as great a delight in burnt offerings and sacrifices as in obeying the voice of the Lord? Behold, to obey is better than sacrifice.   1 SAMUEL 15:22

Weakness

Want of physical strength; want of force or vigor; feebleness

---

When dealing with the pressures of life, you don't have to be overcome or feel overwhelmed. No matter how big your problem appears, you can defeat it with God's help and enjoy victory.

You might think, *I'm just too tired. It seems like I don't have the strength for another battle.* Well, it's actually a good thing to realize you don't have strength for the battle—because if you try to fight in your own strength, you'll lose every time. The only way you are going to really, truly live in victory is by trusting God in your weaknesses, depending completely on Him for strength.

Bring your problems to God—ask Him to help you instead of merely trying in your own strength. Offer your weaknesses to God instead of attempting to hide them and you will find Him filling them with His strength.

When I am weak [in human strength], then am I [truly] strong (able, powerful in divine strength).   2 CORINTHIANS 12:10

Meditate

**To dwell on any thing in thought;
to contemplate; to study**

———————

Meditating on God's Word takes discipline. We live in such a fast-paced world few of us make time to meditate. But it is helpful to set aside time to just sit and think about God's Word and the wonderful promises He made to those who believe in Him.

The blessed person mentioned in Psalm 1:2 is the person who meditates on God's Word "by day and by night." The expression "by day and by night" means it is a major part of a person's life. It's a way of saying that thinking about the Word of God should be a regular part of daily activity.

There are many useless thoughts that try to fill our minds continually, but if we choose to give time to thinking about God's Word it benefits us greatly.

> *But his delight and desire are in the law of the Lord, and on His law (the precepts, the instructions, the teachings of God) he habitually meditates (ponders and studies) by day and by night.*   PSALM 1:2

Crave

To long for as a gratification; to require or demand, as a passion or appetite

---

If we would crave God and go after Him like we do other things, we would have a much more intimate relationship with Him.

God wants to be wanted. He will not push Himself on us. If you want a deeper relationship with God, ask Him to fill you with passion for Him. Perhaps you have never thought about praying to have a passion for what God desires, but it is time to begin.

A half-hearted effort does not build an

intimate relationship with the Lord. He said we are to love Him with our whole heart, soul, mind, and strength (see Matthew 22:37). If that is your true desire, then He will meet you where you are and help you get where you need to be.

Seek, inquire of and for the Lord, and crave Him and His strength (His might and inflexibility to temptation); seek and require His face and His presence [continually] evermore.   PSALM 105:4

Duty

Obedience; submission

We are all going to have an abundance of feelings as long as we are alive, but they are ever changing. Feelings are not at all dependable. You can have feelings, but don't let them cast the final vote in your decision-making.

God speaks in His Word about duty, and it is something that we should not ignore. Sometimes we just need to be determined to obey God because it's the right thing to do and then do our duty as Christians. We don't have to feel like doing a thing in order to do it.

Those who serve in the armed forces

know what this means. They take an oath to "bear true faith and allegiance" to support and defend. They do their duty because it's what they are supposed to do—the right thing to do. As members of the army of God, we can do the same. Our duty is to live as God commands—regardless of our feelings—and to trust God with the results.

I have abundant boldness in Christ to charge you to do what is fitting and required and your duty to do.   PHILEMON 1:8

Restore

To return to a person, as a specific thing which he or she has lost, or which has been taken from the person and unjustly detained

---

Many of us are in a broken-down condition when we finally humble ourselves and ask God to do His work in us. God is a builder and a restorer of what was once lost and destroyed, and He is delighted when we invite Him to restore us.

I had lost a lot of things through the abuse I suffered as a child. I had no confidence and was filled with shame, guilt, bitterness, and many other painful emotions. *But God!* (I love that phrase, which is found in God's Word.) *But God* worked in my life and has rebuilt and restored what was once broken down and useless.

If you feel like you've lost something, you've missed out on something, or are just run down and lacking strength or energy, look to God. He can restore anything you've lost. And He does it abundantly!

Return to the stronghold . . . you prisoners of hope; even today do I declare that I will restore double your former prosperity to you.

ZECHARIAH 9:12

Invited

Requested to come or go in person

One of the first things we ask when invited to a party is, "How should I dress?" Most of us like it best when we feel that we can come as we are. We like it when we can relax and be ourselves.

Romans 1:5–6 says:

It is through Him that we have received grace (God's unmerited favor) and [our] apostleship to promote obedience to the faith and make disciples for His name's sake among all the nations.

And this includes you, called of Jesus Christ
and invited [as you are] to belong to Him.
(Emphasis added)

God will work in you by His Holy
Spirit and help you become all that you
need to be, but you can come to Him just
as you are. You don't have to stand afar and
only hear the music of the party—you are
invited to attend.

And this includes you, called of Jesus Christ
and invited [as you are] to belong to Him.

ROMANS 1:6

Think

To have the mind occupied on some subject; to have ideas, or to revolve ideas in the mind

---

What your life amounts to is directly connected to what you think of yourself. We need to learn to think like God thinks. We must learn to identify with Christ and the new person He has made us to be.

Some identify with the problems they have had in life and call themselves by that name. They say, "I am bankrupt. I am an abuse victim. I am an addict." But they should say, "I *was* bankrupt, but now I am a new creature in Christ. I *was* a victim of abuse, but now I have a new life and a new identity. I *was* an addict, but now I am free, and I have discipline and self-control."

God has a good plan for each of us, but we need to have our minds renewed in order to experience what Jesus has made available for us to enjoy.

> *But God will redeem me ... for He will*
> *receive me. Selah [pause, and calmly think of*
> *that]!*   PSALM 49:15

Peaceful

Quiet; undisturbed; not in a state of war or commotion

God puts different people together and wants us to learn how to love one another and get along peacefully.

God may put a careful, tidy person with a careless, messy person. He may put a strong person with a weak one, a healthy one with a sick one, or a clever person with one who is not so clever. He may put hot-tempered, impatient people together with sweet-tempered and patient people. One of them becomes yoked to the other and God uses them to balance each other out.

This gives us the opportunity to enjoy

and benefit from the strengths of one another. But if we are critical of others because they are not like us, not only will we forfeit peace but we will also miss the opportunity to let their strength fill up our weakness.

Now may the Lord of peace Himself grant you His peace (the peace of His kingdom) at all times and in all ways [under all circumstances and conditions, whatever comes]. The Lord [be] with you all.   2 THESSALONIANS 3:16

Stability

Steadiness; stableness; firmness; strength to stand without being moved or overthrown

---

I think one of the greatest things we can do for people is to be an example of stability to them. We need to be steadfast, consistent, and stable in our lives and behavior.

The world today is such an emotionally charged place, it seems ready to explode at any moment, but that is not God's will for His people.

Jesus said we are in the world, but not of it (see John 17:16). In other words, as believers in Jesus Christ we live in the world, but we should resist acting like it.

We cannot respond the way the world responds to life's situations.

Jesus is our peace; He is the supreme example of stability, and through Him we can enjoy lives of stability, while at the same time being a good example to others.

And there shall be stability in your times,
an abundance of salvation, wisdom, and
knowledge; the reverent fear and worship of
the Lord is your treasure and His.

ISAIAH 33:6

Laughter

Convulsive merriment; an expression of mirth peculiar to man

Laughter is a surefire solution to discouragement. I encourage you to laugh a lot in life because laughter is one source we can always depend on to lift our spirits. It is like internal jogging and is actually very healthy for us.

Maybe you're thinking, *Joyce, there is nothing funny about my life.* If that is the case, then do something funny yourself. Rent a funny movie or visit with someone you know who usually makes you laugh.

I recently spent time with someone

I don't normally spend time with and ended up laughing all evening. I remember thinking, *I didn't know she was that funny, but I am going to make it a habit to be around her more.*

God has created us for work and play, not just work, work, work, and more work! Fun and laughter bring restoration and rest to your soul.

A time to weep and a time to laugh, a time to mourn and a time to dance…

ECCLESIASTES 3:4

Familiar

Well acquainted with; knowing by frequent use

One of the reasons we lose our joy and the freshness and newness of things is familiarity. That simply means we get so accustomed to something we no longer see how special it is.

It's like the mother who started reading the Bible to her young son. A few weeks later they were reading from the Gospel of John. When she read John 3:16, her son commented, "Oh, I know this. This is an old one."

Being familiar with a Scripture can do that to us. We can know it so well we feel we know all there is to know about it. It's the same with the blessings and joys we experience in life. We need to make an effort not to take those things for granted.

If we will determine to daily be in awe of God, His Word and His Presence in our lives, we will avoid the trap of familiarity.

Bless (affectionately, gratefully praise) the Lord, O my soul, and forget not [one of] all His benefits.   PSALM 103:2

Breastplate

Armor for the breast

Jesus did not die for us so we could have a religion. He died so we could be forgiven for our sins, be made right with God, and enjoy fellowship with Him.

Religion is man's attempt to get to a place where God will accept him; it is man's idea of God's expectations. But Christianity is about God taking on humanity in the person of Jesus Christ and coming down to man so we could have relationship with Him.

Righteousness is described in the Bible as a breastplate that covers the heart or spirit of man (see Ephesians 6:14). Our spirits must be covered with righteousness if we are to have rich fellowship with God and walk in victory. God gives us righteousness by His grace, but we are the ones who choose to receive it by faith and walk in it.

Stand therefore [hold your ground], having tightened the belt of truth around your loins and having put on the breastplate of integrity and of moral rectitude and right standing with God.   EPHESIANS 6:14

Determination

Steadfast intention to pursue a purpose

When you have determination in a particular area of your life, Satan may try to steal it, and you will need to talk to yourself in order to keep it.

Sometimes the best way to overcome the temptation to give up on something is to say to yourself, "I refuse to give up. I am going to press through and finish what I have begun."

Over the years, there have been many times I have said to myself: "Joyce, you can make it! It may be hard, but you can make it because God is on your side."

We may not always feel like being determined, but I guarantee that you do not want to risk missing God's will simply because you were not determined to persevere through the difficult times in life.

Now when the time was almost come for Jesus to be received up [to heaven], He steadfastly and determinedly set His face to go to Jerusalem.   LUKE 9:51

View

To survey; to examine with the eye; to look on with attention

---

It is very important to view people the way God views them. In 1 Samuel 16:7, we see how God views us: "For the Lord sees not as man sees; for man looks on the outward appearance, but the Lord looks on the heart." And the Gospels tell us in numerous places that Jesus looked at the crowd and saw them with compassion.

If we are willing, we can learn to think about people the way God thinks about them. Then we'll view each person as a valuable possibility instead of a potential problem.

To see people the way God sees them, and to think about them the way that God thinks about them, comes with spiritual maturity—it is a by-product of walking in the Spirit rather than walking in the flesh. Love always believes the best of all people, and it is our privilege to let God teach us how to do that.

When He saw the throngs, He was moved with pity and sympathy for them, because they were bewildered (harassed and distressed and dejected and helpless), like sheep without a shepherd.   MATTHEW 9:36

Yourself

A word added to "you" to express distinction emphatically between you and other persons

---

I want to ask you a question: Do you like yourself? If not, developing a good relationship with yourself will help you in many ways. You spend every moment of your life with yourself, so it stands to reason that if you don't like yourself, then you will be unhappy and you won't be able to love others the way God loves you.

If you struggle with a poor self-image, with God's help, not only can you think better thoughts about yourself, but you can also take the time to do things for yourself that you enjoy.

God wants us to help others and be available for a wide variety of good works that He has planned; however, if you never take the time to do anything for yourself, you will quickly become burned-out from always giving and never receiving. You will begin to feel that people take advantage of you, but that wrong attitude can be avoided by simply taking time to do things that you enjoy, along with doing things for other people.

And he replied, You must love the Lord your God with all your heart and with all your soul and with all your strength and with all your mind; and your neighbor as yourself.

LUKE 10:27

Influenced

Moved; excited; affected; persuaded; induced

A friend who visits prisons and has spent time with various inmates shared with me that most of the inmates connected the beginnings of their lives of crime to being influenced by the wrong group of people. That shows you the power of influence.

You may not be a negative or a rude person, but if you are around others who are like this for a lengthy period of time, you will start to pick up bad habits. It is like being around people who smoke cigarettes, cigars, or pipes. You may not smoke yourself, but if you're around the smoke, you will end up smelling like smoke anyway.

I encourage you to learn to let God be involved in choosing your friends. This way you will have godly influencers in your life, and you will have friends who make you a better person.

Do not be so deceived and misled! Evil companionships (communion, associations) corrupt and deprave good manners and morals and character.

1 CORINTHIANS 15:33

Build

In scripture, to increase and strengthen; to cement and knit together; to settle or establish and preserve

---

If you're frustrated with the life you've built in your own efforts and feel you need direction, I suggest you turn the construction project over to God. Study His Word, spend time in prayer, learn to listen to His voice, and do what He says.

Trust that God is good and He has a plan for you, and be willing to obey even if He says to stop what you're doing or tells you to do it differently. If you're struggling in your marriage, God may ask *you* to change—even though you want your spouse to change. If you're having financial difficulties, God may tell you to spend less—even though you want Him to give you more. If you're tired and moody, God may tell you to change your diet and get more rest—even though you like your sweets and a hectic schedule. The point is this: If you'll turn the construction of your life over to God, He'll build something beautiful.

Except the Lord builds the house, they labor in vain who build it.   PSALM 127:1

Called

Invited; summoned; addressed; named; appointed; invoked

In the same way Jesus called His disciples to leave their old lives behind and follow Him into something new—something better— He calls you and me to do the same.

The life He has for you is one of promise and victory, full of new things in God, but in order to realize the full potential of that, there will be some things God will call you to walk away from. These are things that you may have grown accustomed to— bad habits, negative thinking, worry, fear, wrong confessions, and so on—but they are things that will imprison you.

You may not eliminate *all* of these bad behaviors from your life right away, but God will lead you daily, step by step, and you will find that as you follow His calling, you will be making progress. God has something better for you. He has new things for you to embrace. Don't wait until tomorrow to obey God—do it today!

God is faithful... by Him you were called into companionship and participation with His Son, Jesus Christ our Lord.

1 CORINTHIANS 1:9

Remember

To preserve the memory of; to preserve from being forgotten

It's good for us to take time to think about all God has done in our lives. If we would remember the miracles God has done in our past, we would not so easily fall into worry and fear when we have new challenges to face.

When David was facing Goliath and nobody was encouraging him, he remembered the lion and the bear that he had already slain with God's help. Because of remembering the victories of his past, he had no fear of the current situation.

Are you facing something right now

that looms before you like a giant in your life? Is it illness or financial lack? Is it a relationship problem? Is it something you have never done before and you don't know where to begin? Whatever it is, nothing is impossible for God. Take some time and recall some of the things God has helped you with and brought you through in the past. Think about and talk about those things and you will find courage filling your heart.

My mouth shall praise You with joyful lips when I remember You upon my bed and meditate on You in the night watches.

PSALM 63:5–6

Approach

Way of addressing a situation

Life is often challenging, and I've discovered that the world around us will not always change, so we must be willing to change our approach to life and the situations we face.

I hear people say things like, "If it rains tomorrow I am not going to be happy," or, "When I get home from work today, I am going to be upset if my children did not clean the house the way I told them to." When we are thinking like this, we are planning to let adverse circumstances steal our joy and control our behavior.

Instead, our approach can be different.

We can say, "I hope the weather is nice tomorrow, but my joy is within me, so I can be happy no matter what kind of weather we have" or, "I hope the children did what I asked them to do so I don't have to correct them, but I can handle any situation and remain peaceful in my soul." It's all a matter of having a more positive, hope-filled approach.

> *Because of our faith in Him, we dare to*
> *have the boldness (courage and confidence)*
> *of free access (an unreserved approach to*
> *God with freedom and without fear).*
>
> EPHESIANS 3:12

Prayer

In worship, a solemn address to the Supreme Being, consisting of adoration, or an expression of our sense of God's glorious perfections, confession of our sins, supplication, intercession for blessings on others, and thanksgiving, or an expression of gratitude to God for his mercies and benefits

---

Our first line of defense against discouragement or disappointment is prayer. The best advice I can give you is to pray at the beginning of each day and each project, and during every trial and disappointment.

Don't merely pray for the situation to go away, but instead pray that you will be able to handle the problem, maintain the character of God, and display the fruit of the Holy Spirit.

Prayer invites the power of God into our lives. It is foolish and a waste of energy and time to try to do anything before praying. Pray at all times, in every season, with every manner of prayer (see Ephesians 6:18). We forfeit more than we can imagine because we often fail to pray. Remember that God wants you to come to Him in faith, trusting Him to meet your needs and accomplish His plans and purposes in your life.

And whatever you ask for in prayer, having faith and [really] believing, you will receive.

MATTHEW 21:22

Amazing

Very wonderful; exciting astonishment, or perplexity

You may not realize this, but as someone who is created in the image of God (see Genesis 1:26–27), you are amazing!

No matter what other people may have told you that you are *not*, God delights in telling you in His Word who you *are* in Him—loved, valuable, precious, talented, gifted, capable, powerful, wise, and redeemed.

I encourage you to take a moment and repeat those nine things out loud. Say, "I am loved, valuable, precious, talented, gifted, capable, powerful, wise, and redeemed through Christ, Who gave His life for me."

God has a good plan for you! Get excited about your life. You are created in God's image and there is no one else on the planet that is exactly like you. You are one of a kind and that makes you valuable. Who you are in Christ is amazing!

But you are a chosen race, a royal priesthood, a dedicated nation, [God's] own purchased, special people.   1 PETER 2:9

Examine

To inspect carefully, with a view to discover truth or the real state of a thing

———————

Have you ever opened your refrigerator door and noticed a bad odor? If so, you probably immediately wondered, *What's that horrible smell?* The only way to eliminate the smell is to find its source. You may cover it up temporarily with some kind of deodorizer, but unless it's completely eliminated, it will always come back.

Sometimes our lives are like that—something stinks. When this happens, we have to examine every aspect of our hearts to find the cause of the problem. Often the source is anger or an offense that we've never dealt with. It lurks in the hidden places of our hearts.

The answer is not for us to cover up an issue, just trying to deodorize the problem. The answer is for us to ask God to help us get to the source, and then help us deal with the problem.

Examine and test and evaluate your own selves to see whether you are holding to your faith and showing the proper fruits of it.

2 CORINTHIANS 13:5

Variety

Deviation; change from a former state

Too much of the ordinary is what we normally get bored with, but I am convinced that it's our own fault. We don't have to wait for something different or exciting to happen to us; we can be aggressive, create variety, and enjoy our lives. Sometimes all bland food needs is a little spice, and it is the same way with our lives.

You don't have to wait for something different to happen to you, but instead you can creatively do something different. Even a small change can bring freshness into what we do.

No day needs to be ordinary if we realize the gift God is giving us when He gives us another day. An extraordinary attitude can quickly turn an ordinary day into an amazing adventure.

> *[The purpose is] that through the church the complicated, many-sided wisdom of God in all its infinite variety and innumerable aspects might now be made known . . . in the heavenly sphere.*   EPHESIANS 3:10

Expectations

**Anticipation that particular events
or outcomes will come to pass**

_____

If you have encountered a lot of disappointments in your life, beware of beginning to expect more of the same.

Sometimes we think we are protecting ourselves from being disappointed if we don't expect anything good to happen. But all that really does is open the door for the devil to keep tormenting us and it closes the door for God to turn things around in our lives.

Create an atmosphere God can work in. He wants to help you; He wants to lift you up and make your life significant.

God wants to heal you and use you to bring healing and restoration into the lives of other hurting people. Isn't that a better expectation to have? Your life can count for something. God has a great plan for you!

For the thing which I greatly fear comes upon me, and that of which I am afraid befalls me.   JOB 3:25

Ambassador

A diplomatic official of the highest rank appointed and accredited as representative in residence by one government or sovereign to another

---

I would like to suggest something for you to add to your daily prayers.

Each day ask God what you can do for Him. Then as you go through your day, watch for opportunities to do what you believe Jesus would do if He were still on the earth in bodily form. Jesus lives in you now if you are a Christian, and you are His ambassador, so make sure you represent Him well.

I spent lots of years in my morning prayers telling the Lord what I needed Him to do for me, but I've learned it's even better to add this part: "God, what is it that I can do for You today?"

So we are Christ's ambassadors, God making His appeal as it were through us. We [as Christ's personal representatives] beg you for His sake to lay hold of the divine favor [now offered you] and be reconciled to God.

2 CORINTHIANS 5:20

Value

Worth; that property or those properties of a thing that render it useful or estimable

---

The fact that God sent His only beloved Son to die a painful death in our place assigns value to us and lets us know God loves us immensely.

The Bible says we are bought with a price, a price that is precious—the blood of Jesus (see 1 Peter 1:19). He paid for our misdeeds, secured our justification, made our account with God balanced, and absolved us from all guilt (see Romans 4:25). Jesus is our substitute. He stood in our place taking what we deserved (punishment as sinners), and freely gave us what He deserves (every kind of blessing).

If you're ever tempted to feel you have no value, just remember all that Jesus did out of His great love for you.

Fear not, then; you are of more value than many sparrows.   MATTHEW 10:31

Inventory

A detailed, itemized list, report, or record of things in one's possession

---

Instead of being unthinking people, we can train ourselves to think about what we are thinking about. If your mood begins to sink, or an attitude is ungodly, take an inventory of your current thoughts, and you will very likely find the culprit.

I enjoy knowing that I can do something about my problems, and I hope that you do also. It is exciting to me to realize that I don't have to sit passively by and let the devil fill my mind with poisonous and destructive thoughts, but that I can learn to inventory and recognize those thoughts.

And by a simple act of my will, I can think about something else that will be beneficial.

When we worry, we let our minds wander, dwelling on what bad thing *might* happen to us. A quick inventory of our thoughts will show us if we are worried and allow us to make a correction to our thoughts.

For the weapons of our warfare are . . . mighty
in God for pulling down strongholds . . .
bringing every thought into captivity to the
obedience of Christ.

2 CORINTHIANS 10:4–5 (NKJV)

First

Preceding all others in order

It's critical for us to realize that God must be our number one priority in every area of our lives. How can we ever hope to have order in our lives if we don't know how to put the most important things first—ahead of everything else?

I tried for many years to work God into my schedule without ever finding the time. Each night I felt guilty because I had failed to spend time with God, and I promised myself the next day would be different, but sadly it was a repeat of the day before. I had good intentions, but procrastination got the better of me.

The answer to my problem was simple, and it's the same answer for yours: Make God the first priority! Take time first thing each day to communicate with your Father in heaven who loves you and wants to be involved in all that you do. If we are too busy for time with God, then we are too busy with things that don't deserve the place of importance we are giving them. If you'll make Him your first priority, everything else will fall into place.

But seek (aim at and strive after) first of all His kingdom and His righteousness... and then all these things taken together will be given you besides. MATTHEW 6:33

Press

To urge with force or weight; a word of extensive use, denoting the application of any power, physical or moral, to something that is to be moved or affected

---

Faith completely turns the tables on your problems. Instead of thinking your problem is too great, you realize that the greater One lives in you (see 1 John 4:4). Instead of being discouraged by difficulties, you begin to laugh at your problems (see Nehemiah 8:10). Instead of feeling anxiety over your situation, you have a bold confidence that God is going to do something amazing (see Proverbs 3:26).

I like to say it this way: "God gives you the strength to press against the pressure that's pressing you!" This is a new mind-set that I encourage you to embrace. Don't be afraid of your problem, don't be stressed-out by your problem, and don't be discouraged by your problem—attack the problem that is attacking you by placing your faith in God.

I press on toward the goal to win the [supreme and heavenly] prize to which God in Christ Jesus is calling us upward.

PHILIPPIANS 3:14

Wonderful

Exciting awe, admiration, or surprise; strange; astonishing

In Genesis 18 Sarah laughed at the thought of having a baby in her old age, and God asked Abraham a powerful question: "Is anything too hard or too wonderful for the Lord?" (Genesis 18:14). That's a question we should remind ourselves of even today.

With God, all things are possible. There is nothing He cannot do. He may do it differently than you planned, and He may do it later than you planned, but His ways and His timing are always better than anything you can imagine.

Take a moment and tell God, "Lord,

I'm open to whatever You have for me. It may not be what I planned, and it may not happen on my timetable, but I trust Your perfect plan for my life. I refuse to give up on You, and I choose to let go of worry, anxiety and fear. I know nothing is too hard or too wonderful for You!"

I will praise You, O Lord, with my whole heart; I will show forth (recount and tell aloud) all Your marvelous works and wonderful deeds!   PSALM 9:1

Comfort

To strengthen the mind when depressed or enfeebled; to console; to give new vigor to the spirits

———————

When I am hurt by someone and I feel angry or upset, it is such a comfort to me to be able to lift my hurt to the Lord, saying, "Jesus, I am so glad You understand what I am feeling right now, and You don't condemn me for feeling this way. I don't want to give vent to my emotions. Help me, Lord, to get over them. Help me forgive those who have wronged me and not slight them, avoid them, or seek to pay them back for the harm they have done me. Heal my emotions and let me feel toward people what You feel."

A prayer like this helps us see that it is not a matter of just thinking, *I shouldn't be feeling this way*; it is a matter of crying out to God and allowing Him to heal our hurts and bring us comfort.

Blessed be the God and Father of our Lord Jesus Christ, the Father... of every comfort (consolation and encouragement).

2 CORINTHIANS 1:3

Mind

**The intellectual or intelligent
power in man; the understanding**

The Word of God tells us that as believers in Jesus, we are given the mind of Christ. That is, we can think spiritual thoughts because Christ is alive within us. We no longer have to think the way we once did. We can begin to think as He did.

Another way to look at this is to point to the promise God spoke through Ezekiel: "A new heart will I give you and a new spirit will I put within you, and I will take away the stony heart out of your flesh and give you a heart of flesh. And I will put my Spirit within you" (Ezekiel 36:26–27).

When we have the Holy Spirit living and active within us, the mind of Christ is in action. The mind of Christ is given to us to direct us in the right way. If we are operating with His mind, we will think positive, life-giving thoughts.

But we have the mind of Christ (the Messiah) and do hold the thoughts (feelings and purposes) of His heart.

1 CORINTHIANS 2:16

Strong

Well fortified; able to sustain attacks; not easily subdued or taken

---

God has equipped and anointed us to do hard things. He allows us to go through difficulty and to bring glory to Him. He shows Himself strong through us. He told Paul that His strength is made perfect in our weakness (see 2 Corinthians 12:9).

We may think we can't make it through difficulty, but those thoughts are inaccurate according to God's Word. He has promised to never allow more to come on us than we can bear (see 1 Corinthians 10:13).

During life's difficulties, one of the thoughts that is usually persistent is, *I can't do this; it is just too much; it is too hard.* Watch out for that type of thinking and when you recognize it, remember that it is a lie. Then replace it with God-inspired thoughts that are something like this: *I can do what I need to do because God is strong in my life.*

> *The name of the Lord is a strong tower; the*
> *[consistently] righteous man . . . runs into it*
> *and is safe, high [above evil] and strong.*
>
> PROVERBS 18:10

Stir

To incite to action; to instigate; to prompt

If you feel stagnant, a major life change may be in order for you, but before you jump ship and run off to start another new thing, make sure you do your part to stir yourself up right where you are.

There are times when we should move on, but I get concerned about people who are constantly starting new things and never finishing anything.

In the Bible, Jesus encountered a man who was ill for thirty-eight years (see John 5:1–9). He had been lying by a pool of water all that time waiting for a miracle.

Jesus' answer to this man's stagnant life was "Get up and get going."

As simple as that sounds, I do believe it is the answer for many people. Stir yourself up!

> *That is why I would remind you to stir up (rekindle the embers of, fan the flame of, and keep burning) the [gracious] gift of God.*
>
> 2 TIMOTHY 1:6

Little

Small in size or extent; not great or large

It's easy to overlook the importance of being faithful in the little things in life. We need to remember to do little things that potentially have big power. So often, when we think of making a difference in life, we think of big undertakings, and we wonder how in the world we'll accomplish them. But little things can be just as effective, if not more powerful.

- A hug or a smile can change someone's day.

- Showing appreciation can save a marriage.
- An extra five minutes at work every night could mean you are the one who doesn't get laid off.
- Saying little prayers all throughout the day can bring you closer to God.
- Letting someone else with fewer groceries go in front of you in line could create an opportunity to share your testimony.

Little things done each day can change the course of someone's life completely.

He who is faithful in a very little [thing] is faithful also in much, and he who is dishonest and unjust in a very little [thing] is dishonest and unjust also in much.   LUKE 16:10

Ownership

The state or fact of being an owner

When offenses come and we are tempted to get into strife, it is wise for us to examine our thoughts and take ownership of our actions.

If you find that you are justifying having a bad attitude, I encourage you to realize that justifying any bad behavior that the Word of God condemns is a dangerous thing. It keeps us deceived and unable to take ownership of our faults.

Nobody enjoys saying, "I was wrong—please forgive me," but it is one of the most powerful six-word sentences in the world. It brings peace to turmoil; joy replaces frustration and this attitude puts a smile on God's face. He is delighted when we follow His ways instead of our own thoughts, feelings, and behaviors.

But let every person carefully scrutinize and examine and test his own conduct and his own work.   GALATIANS 6:4

Wanted

Needed; desired

We have been chosen by God, picked out as His own in Christ before the foundation of the world (see Ephesians 1:4). Before we had an opportunity to do anything right or wrong, God decided He wanted us!

I want to encourage you to really think about how wonderful it is to be loved and wanted by God. This means we can relax and receive God's love. We can think about it, thank Him for it, and watch for the manifestation of it in our daily lives.

God shows His love for us in many ways, but we are often unaware of it. He loves us first, so we can love Him and other people. God never expects us to give away something that He has not first given us. His love is poured out into our hearts by the Holy Spirit, and He wants us to live before Him in love.

And He went up on the hillside and called to Him [for Himself] those whom He wanted and chose, and they came to Him.

MARK 3:13

Encourage

To give courage to; to give or increase confidence of success; to inspire with courage, spirit, or strength of mind; to embolden

---

One of the best things we can be is an encourager. Rather than discourage those around us with negativity or cynicism, we can actually look for ways to be a constant source of inspiration and encouragement.

Everyone loves to be with people who celebrate and notice their strengths and choose to overlook their weaknesses. We all love to be encouraged and made to feel really good about ourselves, and we dislike being around negative people who tend to be faultfinders.

The more you encourage people, the better they will be. In fact, compliments actually help people rise to their potential, while nagging drags them down. Choose a person whom you would like to have a better relationship with and begin to aggressively encourage him or her.

Therefore encourage (admonish, exhort) one another and edify (strengthen and build up) one another.   1 THESSALONIANS 5:11

Pleased

**Gratified; affected with agreeable
sensations or emotions**

One of the miraculous benefits of being a
child of God is knowing that He is pleased
with us.

In Scripture, God uses words like "beautiful," "honored," "valued," and "precious"
when He is speaking of His people. There is
no doubt that we are less than perfect, that
we have faults and weaknesses. We make
mistakes and bad choices and often lack wisdom, but God is God, and He views us the
way He knows we can be.

God sees us as a finished project while
we are making the journey. He sees the

end from the beginning and is not worried about what takes place in between. God is not pleased with sin or bad behavior, but He will never give up on us. When He sees us, He sees that we are righteous because of the sacrifice of His Son, Jesus, and He is pleased.

> *Glory to God in the highest [heaven], and on earth peace among men with whom He is well pleased [men of goodwill, of His favor].*
>
> LUKE 2:14

Forgiveness

The pardoning of an offender

———————

I am continually amazed by the number of people I encounter who love God and are trying to move forward with Him while still harboring anger, unforgiveness, or other negative emotions in their hearts.

Sometimes they are angry with someone for a situation or offense that happened many years ago. They often say, "Well, I have really tried to get over this, but I just can't."

Yes, they can (and yes, you can). God never asks us to do anything impossible. If He tells us to forgive, then we can forgive. If He tells us not to be offended, then there is a way for us to keep from being offended. It's not always easy, and we're going to need His help, but the truth is we can forgive that person who hurt us and we can live free of bitterness, anger, and unforgiveness.

Be gentle and forbearing with one another and, if one has a difference (a grievance or complaint) against another, readily pardoning each other; even as the Lord has [freely] forgiven you, so must you also [forgive].

COLOSSIANS 3:13

Perseverance

Persistence in any thing undertaken; continued pursuit or prosecution of any business or enterprise begun

---

I believe one of the most important traits a Christian can have is perseverance. A persistent Christian is a prepared and powerful Christian.

Persistence is vital because there are going to be difficulties in life. The Bible never promised that when you gave your life to God, you'd no longer have any problems. As I'm sure you've noticed, life isn't always a cakewalk; there are going to be difficult days and trying circumstances, but going through them instead of giving up is what makes us strong.

When you know who you are in God and trust the power of the Holy Spirit within you, you don't give up when things get tough—you persevere.

> *[We pray] that you may be invigorated and strengthened with all power according to the might of His glory, [to exercise] every kind of endurance and patience (perseverance and forbearance) with joy.*   COLOSSIANS 1:11

Do you have a real relationship with Jesus?

God loves you! He created you to be a special, unique, one-of-a-kind individual, and He has a specific purpose and plan for your life. And through a personal relationship with your Creator—God—you can discover a way of life that will truly satisfy your soul.

No matter who you are, what you've done, or where you are in your life right now, God's love and grace are greater than your sin—your mistakes. Jesus willingly gave His life so you can receive forgiveness from God and have new life in Him. He's just waiting for you to invite Him to be your Savior and Lord.

If you are ready to commit your life to Jesus and follow Him, all you have to do is ask Him to forgive your sins and give you a fresh start in the life you are meant to live. Begin by praying this prayer...

Lord Jesus, thank You for giving Your life for me and forgiving me of my sins so I can have a personal relationship with You. I am sincerely sorry for the mistakes I've made, and I know I need You to help me live right.

Your Word says in Romans 10:9, "If you declare with your mouth, 'Jesus is Lord,' and believe in your heart that God raised him from the dead, you will be saved" (NIV). I believe You are the Son of God and confess You as my Savior and Lord. Take me just as I am, and work in my heart, making me the person You want me to be. I want to live for You, Jesus, and I am so grateful that You are giving me a fresh start in my new life with You today.

I love You, Jesus!

It's so amazing to know that God loves us so much! He wants to have a deep, intimate relationship with us that grows every day as we spend time with Him in prayer and Bible study. And we want to encourage you in your new life in Christ.

Please visit joycemeyer.org/salvation to request Joyce's book *A New Way of Living*, which is our gift to you. We also have other free resources online to help you make progress in pursuing everything God has for you.

Congratulations on your fresh start in your life in Christ! We hope to hear from you soon.

About the Author

JOYCE MEYER is one of the world's leading practical Bible teachers. Her daily broadcast, *Enjoying Everyday Life*, airs on hundreds of television networks and radio stations worldwide.

Joyce has written more than one hundred inspirational books. Her bestsellers include *Power Thoughts*; *The Confident Woman*; *Look Great, Feel Great*; *Starting Your Day Right*; *Ending Your Day Right*; *Approval Addiction*; *How to Hear from*

God; *Beauty for Ashes*; and *Battlefield of the Mind*.

Joyce travels extensively, holding conferences throughout the year and speaking to thousands around the world.

JOYCE MEYER MINISTRIES
U.S. & Foreign Office Addresses

Joyce Meyer Ministries

P.O. Box 655
Fenton, MO 63026
USA
(636) 349-0303

Joyce Meyer Ministries—Canada

P.O. Box 7700
Vancouver, BC V6B 4E2
Canada
(800) 868-1002

Joyce Meyer Ministries—Australia

Locked Bag 77
Mansfield Delivery Centre
Queensland 4122
Australia
(07) 3349 1200

Joyce Meyer Ministries—England

P.O. Box 1549
Windsor SL4 1GT
United Kingdom
01753 831102

Joyce Meyer Ministries—South Africa

P.O. Box 5
Cape Town 8000
South Africa
(27) 21-701-1056

Other Books by Joyce Meyer

100 Ways to Simplify Your Life
21 Ways to Finding Peace and Happiness
Any Minute
Approval Addiction
The Approval Fix
The Battle Belongs to the Lord
Battlefield of the Mind*
Battlefield of the Mind for Kids
Battlefield of the Mind for Teens
Battlefield of the Mind Devotional
Be Anxious for Nothing*
Being the Person God Made You to Be
Beauty for Ashes
Change Your Words, Change Your Life
The Confident Mom
The Confident Woman
The Confident Woman Devotional
Do Yourself a Favor . . . Forgive
Eat the Cookie . . . Buy the Shoes
Eight Ways to Keep the Devil Under Your Feet
Ending Your Day Right
Enjoying Where You Are on the Way to Where You Are Going
The Everyday Life Bible
Filled with the Spirit

Get Your Hopes Up!
Good Health, Good Life
Hearing from God Each Morning
*How to Hear from God**
How to Succeed at Being Yourself
I Dare You
*If Not for the Grace of God**
In Pursuit of Peace
The Joy of Believing Prayer
Knowing God Intimately
A Leader in the Making
Life in the Word
Living Beyond Your Feelings
Living Courageously
Look Great, Feel Great
Love Out Loud
The Love Revolution
Making Good Habits, Breaking Bad Habits
Making Marriage Work (previously published as *Help Me—I'm Married!*)
*Me and My Big Mouth!**
*The Mind Connection**
Never Give Up!
Never Lose Heart
New Day, New You
*Overload**
The Penny

Perfect Love (previously published as
God Is Not Mad at You)*

The Power of Being Positive

The Power of Being Thankful

The Power of Determination

The Power of Forgiveness

The Power of Simple Prayer

Power Thoughts

Power Thoughts Devotional

Power Words

Reduce Me to Love

The Secret Power of Speaking God's Word

The Secrets of Spiritual Power

The Secret to True Happiness

Seven Things That Steal Your Joy

Start Your New Life Today

Starting Your Day Right

Straight Talk

Teenagers Are People Too!

Trusting God Day by Day

The Word, the Name, the Blood

Woman to Woman

You Can Begin Again

Joyce Meyer Spanish Titles

Belleza en Lugar de Cenizas (Beauty for Ashes)

Buena Salud, Buena Vida (Good Health, Good Life)

Cambia Tus Palabras, Cambia Tu Vida
(*Change Your Words, Change Your Life*)
El Campo de Batalla de la Mente (*Battlefield of the Mind*)
Como Formar Buenos Habitos y Romper Malos Habitos
(*Making Good Habits, Breaking Bad Habits*)
La Conexión de la Mente (*The Mind Connection*)
Dios No Está Enojado Contigo (*God Is Not Mad at You*)
La Dosis de Aprobación (*The Approval Fix*)
Empezando Tu Día Bien (*Starting Your Day Right*)
Hazte Un Favor a Ti Mismo . . . Perdona (*Do Yourself a
Favor . . . Forgive*)
Madre Segura de sí Misma (*The Confident Mom*)
Palabras de Poder (*Power Words*)
Pensamientos de Poder (*Power Thoughts*)
Sobrecarga (*Overload*)
Termina Bien tu Día (*Ending Your Day Right*)
Usted Puede Comenzar de Nuevo (*You Can Begin Again*)
¡Viva con Esperanza! (*Get Your Hopes Up!*)
Viva Valientemente (*Living Courageously*)

Books by Dave Meyer

Life Lines

* Study Guide available for this title